D1561759

ST. CHARLES
AT CHARLESTOWN

Author in front of Resurrection Chapel
at The Sharon Johnston Park

Courtesy The Huntsville Times, Nov. 16, 1986,
P. B1 and BJ13, Fighting Back; Lucile Johnston Wages
a Crusade to Save Our Cultural Roots by Dale James

CELEBRATIONS OF A NATION
Early American Holidays

by Lucile Johnston

CELEBRATIONS

OF A

NATION

Early American Holidays

LUCILE JOHNSTON

JOHNSTON BICENTENNIAL FOUNDATION
CRYSTAL TOWERS, 1209N
1600 S. Eads St.
Arlington, VA 22202
703-920-1987

DEDICATION

This book is gratefully dedicated to my daughter, Gretl Johnston and my son, Barry Johnston, who cheered me on when the going got rough and gave me my first word processor; to Dall Shady, who guided me through the wilderness of word processor technology and rescued me more times than I can remember; to the writers and artists who went before and recorded the facts as acknowledged in my Bibliography, References, and Illustrations; to the National Thanksgiving Foundation who accepted it as their Official Bicentennial Publication and included me in their efforts to restore an attitude of gratitude in this nation; and to the many friends who encouraged me and prayed for me as I sought to remind the United States of the vision and covenants of our founding fathers and the blessings of a nation *whose God is the Lord* and whose motto is *In God We Trust*.

Year of Thanksgiving Bicentennial Edition

To Brian Roquemore
With best wishes, Ronald Reagan

On February 12, 1987, President Ronald Reagan signed a proclamation designating 1987 as the National Year of Thanksgiving to commemorate 200 years of freedom under the United States Constitution.

Celebrations of a Nation has been adopted as the official publication of the National Year of Thanksgiving Foundation because it is an accurate and readable history of how we came to have this great heritage we will be celebrating on September 17, 1987, followed by the bicentennial of the beginning of our present Government and the inauguration of our first president in 1989 and the adoption of The Bill of Rights in 1991.

Let us thank the God of our Pilgrim fathers that it is not too late to learn from those courageous people who, like us, lived in a confused generation.

Let us thank Him for the signers of *The Declaration of Independence* who saw the battle for what it was and had the courage to trust in God to see them through. And let us be grateful for George Washington whose unswerving faith in and obedience to God carried us to victory and a sound government under *The Constitution* and *Bill of Rights*.

Please call or write us for low quantity prices and help us distribute this book that all Americans might know and appreciate our unique Judeo-Christian heritage.

Yours in the love of our country,

Lucile Johnston

Johnston Bicentennial Foundation
Crystal Towers, 1209N
1600 S. Eads St.
Arlington, VA 22202
703-920-1987

Table of Contents

Thanksgiving--
The First American Holiday

The First Thanksgiving, J.L.C. Ferris Archives of 76, Bay Village, Ohio

CHAPTER ONE

Who Were These Pilgrims?

Thanksgiving today is more like a Roman Holiday than the Holy Day that was celebrated by the Pilgrims in the fall of 1621, almost a year after that stormy, tortuous voyage of the *Mayflower* to the rugged coast of New England.

The football games, the Thanksgiving sales in our shopping malls, the Macy Parade, the early Christmas decorations that crowd out the less commercial symbols of Thanksgiving, the deliberate erasure of our Judeo-Christian history from our textbooks, historical fiction, TV, and movies--all contribute to the growing ignorance of our first American holiday.

Not knowing our history, and basing our beliefs on historical fiction and distorted textbooks, Americans have been gullible enough to think we were learning our heritage. As a result, we have become fair game for all who seek to destroy the freedoms that were so important to the Pilgrims--the most influential and, in our era, the least understood people our nation has ever known.

And yet I have found the story of the Pilgrims, as recorded by them, to be far more interesting and exciting than all the historical fiction and distorted textbooks I have read.

History classes were very boring and difficult for me because I hated memorizing the names and dates, and I never understood the significance of what was taking place. But when, as State Coordinator for the Freedom Council, I was challenged to compare the original documents with what is being taught today, and began to read our forefather's account of what had really happened and why, I became excited and highly motivated to learn what had made my country the greatest and best on earth.

As a member of my State Ad Hoc Textbook Committee on Social Studies, I came to agree with Dr. Paul Vitz, who was given a $70,000 grant by the Department of Education and, after researching many textbooks, reported there was no mention of Protestantism and no mention of our Judeo-Christian heritage. He is a Catholic, but concerned over the distortion of our history.

The new textbooks have erased the very idea of human freedom and our children will never learn from them what our founding fathers paid such a great price to obtain for us. Nor will they be able to judge for themselves what will secure or endanger their freedom.

What is the truth about our real history? Fortunately, the Archives of America, the Rare Books Division of the Library of Congress, and other archives and libraries, still give us the answer to this question. Like the Pilgrims we can believe the promise of Jesus, John 8:31, "If you continue in my word, then are ye my disciples indeed; and ye shall know the truth, and the truth shall make you free."

In fact, I am becoming more and more aware it was the Pilgrim's devotion to the truth that played a crucial role in making us free in the beginning of this nation, and that these truths have continued to keep us free. That is, until a few humanists in our courts, congress, media, bureaucracy, and educational system, like termites, began to eat away at our foundations, while most of us have not realized the freedoms we all enjoy so much are being stolen from us.

My study of their writings from the original documents tell me these Pilgrims we know so little about, in the crucible of suffering, near starvation, and the threat of hostile forces, worked out enduring principles that not only built this nation upon a rock, but could help us solve the mushrooming problems that are undermining our families and our nation today. The price we are paying for not learning from them may be the very freedoms we Americans have always valued so highly.

If this be true, doesn't it then follow we should study the lives and writings of these people who, along with their descendants, played such a vital role in the establishment of this land of liberty? We may find this precious liberty for which the Pilgrims gave their all, has been turned into license because we have forgotten what liberty really means.

4

We may discover, as they did, who the real enemy of mankind is. They knew him to be the devil who, John 10:10, "...comes to kill, steal, and destroy."

Hopefully, we may become as highly motivated as they to find the joyous and abundant life they were seeking and succeeded in finding in this wilderness beyond the sea...a life that was eventually to draw people from every part of the globe, but which is threatened in our time as never before.

Who were these Pilgrims who gave us our first American Holiday? How did these forty-seven brave men, women, and children change the course of human history? What motivated them to risk everything for the hard and dangerous venture of settling this new land?

It all began with an Englishman by the name of Wycliffe, who was called "The Morning Star of the Reformation." In an age of darkness, filled with anti-Christian idolatry, this wonderful man wrote almost two hundred books. But, more important, about one hundred and thirty years before the Reformation of Martin Luther, he translated the scriptures into English and taught the people to read so they could know for themselves what God had to say to them in *The Holy Bible*.

His love of truth, freedom, and independence moved him to give his countrymen the open Scripture as their best hope, safeguard, and protection. He truly believed this book in the hands of a literate people would make possible freedom and self-government for all who obeyed its precepts.

Reading it, the people of England discovered that, in the beginning, Christianity was simply the Gospel of Christ's death in payment for their personal sins and the sins of the whole world and his resurrection to rule in the kingdom he had taught them was at hand and within when they accepted Him as their Lord and Saviour. They learned the early churches began as believers were drawn together by God's Spirit in them, by the good news Jesus had taught them of the kingdom of God, and by their love for God and each other.

They also discovered that the society of believers in Christ was a little republic--people who elected their representatives from the

5

most godly men among them. They learned the first century churches were local institutions composed of self-governing individuals responsible to Christ for their character and the character of those in their fellowship.

This knowledge inevitably led to disenchantment with the Roman Church and the "Divine Rights of Kings." Accustomed to translating the Bible from Latin and interpreting it for the people, the clergy was threatened by the fact that the people were now able to read and interpret God's Word for themselves--many of them better than the unconverted priests, for it is spiritually discerned and many of the priests were not born of the Spirit of God and had no spiritual discernment. The king was threatened as the people became aware that Jesus alone was their king.

This brought the wrath of the church and king down on them and, in 1408, the Provincial Council of Oxford prohibited English translations of the Bible on pain of excommunication and trial for heresy. In 1425, forty-one years after his death, all of Wycliff's books were ordered burned, but his doctrine remained and his disciples, who were called Lollards, continued to teach the English people to read the Bible, resulting in a spiritual awakening for those who believed. Their study of, and obedience to, God's Word eventually led to the coming of the Pilgrims to America.[1]

The real father of our present English Bible was Tyndale, a superb scholar who translated his Bible from the original Hebrew and Greek. (Wycliff's translation had been from the Roman Catholic Latin translation.)

It has been said that, for felicity of diction and dignity of rhythm, Tyndale has never been surpassed and that 80 percent of our Old Testament and 90 percent of our new are directly from his work. It was a labor of love while in exile from the England he so "loved and longed for," with the almost certain penalty of violent death hanging over his head if he returned.

He published the New Testament in 1525 and began his translation of the Old Testament, completing Joshua to II Chronicles. In 1534 he brought out a revised edition of the Pentateuch and the New Testament and, having returned to England, was betrayed and martyred in the spring of the following year.[2]

Burned at stake for his excellent English translation of *The Bible,* Tyndale died praying for his king, the notorious Henry VIII. His death was not in vain. Within a year after his martyrdom, his translation--which had been burned at St. Paul's Cathedral-- was formally approved by the King he had prayed for while the flames swept around him.[3]

The Matthew Bible, which was actually a copy of Tyndale's translation together with Coverdale's, was published under the shelter of a royal proclamation and license in 1536. Henry VIII wanted a divorce from his Catholic wife and an Anglican church under himself instead of under the Pope. Having been advised the Bible would help him wean the people from the Pope, he issued an injunction ordering all clergy to provide "...one bok of the whole Bible, in the largest volume, in Englishe, set up in summe convenyent place within the churche that ye have care of, whereat your parishioners may most commodiously resort to the same and rede yt..."[4]

First forbidden, then silently tolerated, and next licensed, it was now commanded by the King to be set up for the benefit of the eleven thousand parishes in the land!

This "Great Bible" was a magnificent specimen of the art of printing, with a frontispiece said to be designed by Hans Holbein, but it was unwieldy and designed primarily for church use.[5]

The most prized possession of the Pilgrims was *The Geneva Bible.* It was produced by anonymous English Protestants who were exiled in Geneva, Switzerland--a city reputed to be the best place to learn of Christ in that day because of the teaching there of the brilliant French theologian, John Calvin. They stated they were motivated to prepare a new translation to help Christians to walk in fear and love of God and that this would be best done when one had a knowledge of the Word of God."

A Bible for the people, it was smaller, less expensive, and the first Bible to be divided into verses and to provide marginal commentary "upon all the hard places." Commentary and explanation preceded each book and each chapter of *The Bible,* and "the chief point of the page" was at the top of each page. It also included maps and a table of principal things and other help for a layman wanting to study God's Word.

From the beginning *The Geneva Bible* was appointed to be read in the churches of Scotland. Immediately the most popular book in England, it was published in over 120 editions before the incomparable King James Authorized Version of the Bible appeared in 1611, and in over 60 editions afterwards.[6]

As the people read the Bible, they realized everything that is taking place in the world is either in the will of God or the result of going against His Word and following false gods. They saw that God clearly lays down principles to follow in all the basic institutions of society--the family, the school, the church, the government and the economic system. Becoming aware of how far the church of their day had come from the precepts and examples of the first-century church, they began to protest.

By the seventeenth century these Protestants, as they were called, came under increasingly heavy attack. Stern penalties were imposed on all who refused to give allegiance to the national church in England.

The Puritans were a group of probably less than a thousand people trying to reform the Church of England from within. They were pioneers in searching the Scripture for answers to all aspects of life in which man was engaged, including government.

The Pilgrims were Puritans who despaired of bringing about reformation in the Church of England and began their own independent churches. All were persecuted, but the heaviest punishment fell on those who advocated splitting off from the national Anglican Church. These--pitifully few in number--were persecuted, robbed of their possessions, and hounded out of the country. But God meant it for good! He destined them to become pioneers in a larger enterprise--the taking of the gospel to America and the world.

Their Governor and historian wrote, "...a great hope & inward zeal they had of laying some good foundation, or at least to make some way thereunto, for ye propagating & advancing ye gospell of ye kingdom of Christ in those remote parts of ye world; yea, though they should be but even as stepping-stones unto others for ye performing of so great a work."[7]

They saw themselves as steppingstones, and that is exactly what they were, for the Christian civil freedom they began in America, which culminated in the United States, was not to be for one race, one kind of people, or one nationality, but for all who were willing to accept Jesus Christ as their Saviour and his internal government as the source and root of self-government, and to work out their lives in obedience to His Word.

Their faith in God, the Father, and in Jesus Christ, His Son, and obedience to the Bible and the leading of the Holy Spirit resulted in Christian self-government. This was the foundation of the Pilgrim colony from the beginning, and they never found any reason to believe that "...government of the people, by the people, and for the people..." as envisioned by Wycliff would work without this foundation John Calvin, and other reformers gave them. And so it was with the Reformation motto, *Sola Scriptura--The Bible the only measure of truth*--the English colonies took root in what came to mean for many even to this present day the New Promised Land.

Embarkation of Pilgrims, 1620, by Robt. W. Weir, Capitol Rotunda

CHAPTER TWO

Why Did These Pilgrims Come to Plymouth Rock?

Actually, the Pilgrims had no intention of coming to Plymouth Rock, but they finally concluded God intended it. After over three months at sea they were hardly ready to turn back, and they couldn't sail south to Virginia as they had intended because of the rough seas that threatened to smash them on the rock-bound northern coast.

Puritans who wished to separate from the Church of England, they had been hounded out of the country. Leaving friends and possessions behind, they had sailed for Holland, and were thenceforth known as Pilgrims. They finally settled in Leyden where they were welcome because of their honesty and industry and were free to worship together according to their understanding of *The Bible*.

However, they only remained twelve years because in Holland there was a very great problem for them: they were forbidden to share their faith with others. This put them "between the rock and a hard place," for they took seriously the words of Jesus, "All power is given unto me in heaven and in earth. Go ye therefore, and teach all nations, baptizing them in the name of the Father, and of the Son, and of the Holy Ghost; teaching them to observe all things whatsoever I have commanded you: and lo, I am with you always even unto the end of the world."[1]

Also, they were exhausted by 14-hour work days and concerned that their children were being influenced by the materialistic Dutch people.

The answer to their dilemma soon came. In the new world an English colony had been established with the *Virginia Charter* which read:

"We, greatly commending and graciously accepting of the desires of the furtherance of so noble a work, which may by the providence of almighty God hereafter tend to the glory of His divine majesty, *in propagating of Christian religion to such people as yet live in darkness and miserable ignorance of the true knowledge and worship of God, and may in time bring the infidels and savages living in those parts, to human civility and to a settled and quiet government...*"[2]

They could go to America where, under this Virginia Charter, they would be free "...in propagating of Christian religion..." This would enable them to fulfill their covenant with God and each other. As God had called Abraham out of Ur and made a covenant with him to give him and his descendants the land of the Canaanites, the Hittites, the Amorites, the Perizzites, the Jubusites and the Girgashites, they believed they were children of Abraham by faith and called into the same covenant relationship as Israel had to go to this "New Promised Land."[3]

God had prepared them for the dangerous voyage to America with in-depth Bible study back in England at Scrooby, where William Brewster and William Bradford taught them the lessons of truth and freedom. Their Pastor, John Robinson, later wrote, "Here they acquired the moral and spiritual courage which enabled them to sacrifice their homes, property, and friends, and expatriate themselves to distant lands, rather than abandon their principles and yield to the attempted usurpations of the liberty of their consciences."[4]

Like the children of Israel in the Egyptian brick yards before they left for the Promised Land, these Pilgrims had been put through a physical fitness program during the long years of hard labor in Holland, and so were hardier and more accustomed to work than the Virginians who settled Jamestown--some of whom refused to work at all, resulting in 90 percent dying of starvation and disease.

In addition, they had grown in faith by individually and collectively studying and acting on the Word of God and had developed a strong fellowship like that of the first-century church as they underwent trials and persecution together in England and dangers, imprisonment, and loss of possessions before coming to Holland where they learned to work in harmony. All these trials were to contribute to their survival and well-being in the new land.

As the Leyden Pilgrims sailed from Holland to England on the first leg of their voyage to America, they knew they were Pilgrims, and "...lifted up their eyes to the heavens, their dearest country, and quieted their spirits."[5]

Robert Cushman and John Carver had gone ahead to make arrangements with Thomas Weston and to obtain partial backing for their venture. While Carver was out of London gathering supplies, Cushman yielded to Weston's pressure and agreed to changes in their contract without the knowledge or consent of the others.

They were aboard the *Speedwell* and the *Mayflower,* the two ships they had bargained for, and ready to sail when Weston sprung these changes on the Pilgrims. They refused to agree and he angrily left without settling their remaining debts. The Pilgrims were forced to sell several thousand pounds of precious butter in order to leave with their conscience "clear as their credit balance."[6]

On the 21st of July, 1620, the Pilgrims observed a day of humiliation and prayer and listened to their pastor, John Robinson, preach on Ezra 8: 21-22: "Then I proclaimed a fast there, at the river of Ahava, that we might afflict ourselves before our God, to seek of him a right way for us and for our little ones, and for all our substance...we have spoken unto the king, saying, The hand of our God is upon all of them for good that seek Him; but his power and his wrath is against all them that forsake Him."

Robinson had put his fine education at Cambridge University and his career in the church on the altar, confessing,"...had not the truth been in my heart as a burning fire shut up in my bones...I had suffered the light of God to have been put out in mine own unthankful heart by other men's darkness." Now he reminded them of "...our church covenant, at least that part of it whereby we promise and covenant with God and one another to receive whatsoever light or truth shall be made known to us from his written Word; but withal exhorted us to take heed what we received from truth, and well to examine and compare it and weigh it with other Scriptures of truth before we received it. For saith he, it is not possible the Christian world should come so lately out of such thick antichristian darkness, and that full perfection of knowledge should break forth at once."[7]

The *Speedwell* twice had trouble at sea, and twice returned to port. (As the ship remained in service for many years afterward, some historians have suggested the captain may have deliberately put stress on his ship in order to cause the seams to leak because he didn't want to fulfill his risky contract with them.)

Finally, all were transferred to the *Mayflower*. Twenty passengers dropped out, including Robert Cushman who wrote to a friend explaining, "For besides the eminent dangers of this voyage, which are no less than deadly...Our victuals will be half eaten up, I think, before we go from the coast of England, and if our voyage last long, we shall not have a month's victuals when we come (to) the country...Friend, if ever we make a plantation, God works a miracle."[8]

Later historians wrote, "God sifted a whole nation that He might send choice grain into this wilderness."[9]

"Like Gideon's army this small number was divided, as if the Lord, by this work of His Providence, thought these few were still too many for the great work He had to do," wrote William Bradford, the historian of the Pilgrims.[10]

On August 5, 1620, one hundred and two people finally sailed on the *Mayflower* from Plymouth, England, enduring over three months of misery in the hold of this little ship. Sixteen men, eleven women, and fourteen children were from Leyden and there were only forty-seven Pilgrims in all on the ship.[11] The rest were recruited by Weston and the "Merchant Adventurers" who helped finance the voyage. While some were responsible people, others turned out to be troublemakers--"tares planted by the devil in the Lord's vineyard."[12]

Their Captain Jones bore the Christian name of Christopher, which means "Christ-bearer," like another west-bound captain-- Christopher Columbus. He was Christ-like enough to give his cabin to the women and children and bunk with his officers.

Imagine the trials of those courageous Pilgrims and fellow voyagers, enduring over three months of heat, storm, anger, fear, and despair in the crowded, lantern-lit hold of the *Mayflower;* forced by violent storms to stay below and keep the hatches closed; existing on a diet of dried pork, peas, and fish; overwhelmed by the increasingly foul air of the bilge; and oppressed by the crying of little children. Not the least of their trials was the mocking of the sailors. It subsided, however, after the one most vocal in saying he could hardly wait to wrap them in shrouds and toss them to the sharks suddenly came down with a fever and died within a day. He was the first of only two to be wrapped in shrouds and tossed overboard during the entire voyage. The other, refusing to drink the lemon juice provided daily to prevent it, died of scurvy.[13]

Their faith had been built during the voyage by the amazing rescue of John Howland, a servant of John Carver. Disobeying the Captain's orders, he had gone topside to escape the stench below and been swept overboard. One of the spars from the ship was trailing in the icy water as the ship heeled over in his direction, and "happened to snake across his wrist. He closed on it and instinctively hung on." Blue and very sick, he was hauled aboard and to their amazement miraculously recovered.[14]

When the crossbeam supporting the main mast broke during a violent storm, the Pilgrims not only prayed but dug out the heavy iron screw from Brewster's printing press and used it to lift the mast back in place and hold it. After that the sailors and other passengers not only quieted down, in gratitude for the Pilgrims having saved the ship, but joined them in praising God.

On November 9, 1620, driven off course by violent storms, the weary passengers heard the welcome cry, "Land Ho!" and all rushed topside for their first sight of Cape Cod--far north of their original destination. After almost crashing on the dangerous reefs as they struggled to sail south for the Virginia Colony, the Pilgrims reluctantly concluded the Lord would have them settle on this bleak and inhospitable shore.

That month their historian, William Bradford, wrote, "...For summer being done, all things stand upon them with a weather-beaten face; and ye whole countrie, full of woods & thickets, represented a wild & savage heiw...having passed the vast ocean and a sea of troubles before in their preparation, they have now no friends to welcome them...no houses or much less towns...And for the season, it was winter....What could now sustain them but the Spirit of God and His grace? May not and ought not the children of these fathers rightly say, Our fathers were Englishmen which came over this great ocean, and were ready to perish in this wilderness, but they cried unto the Lord and He heard their voice and looked on their adversity, & c. Let them therefore praise ye Lord, because he is good, & his mercies endure forever. Let them which have been redeemed of ye Lord shew how he hath delivered them from ye hand of ye oppressour. When they wandered in ye desert wildernes out of ye way, and found no citie to dwell in, both hungrie, & thirstie, their sowle was overwhelmed in them. Let them confess before ye Lord his loving kindness, and his wonderful works before ye sons of men."[15]

From the beginning, having no response from their request for a document guaranteeing them religious freedom, they had felt doubts as to their really having the freedom they had come for. With no alternative, they had concluded they would have to rest on God's Providence. This must be His provision for them!

The Mayflower Compact, 1620, J.L.G. Ferris, Archives of 76, Bay Village, Ohio

CHAPTER THREE

Why Was The Mayflower Compact So Important?

Before they landed, realizing they were no longer under the Virginia Charter, the Pilgrims drew up the historic *Mayflower Compact*. William Bradford's copy, preserved in his handwriting in his history Of *Plimouth Plantation*, showed only eleven signatures, but an official publication of the Plymouth Colonies in l669 bore the signatures of forty-one men.[1]

This *Compact* was very important because, for the first time in recorded history, free and equal men voluntarily, in writing, covenanted with God and each other to create their own civil government. It turned out to be the forerunner of *The Declaration of Independence,* but even more important in its historic signficance is a little known fact today, but one of which the Pilgrims, great students of the Bible, must have been aware: It was the first time since the Israelites chose to have a king instead of allowing God to rule over them that man had any other government except man over man.

God had warned His people through His servant, Samuel, that the result of going from a theocracy to a kingdom would be great human misery.[2]

For almost 3000 years, from 1120 B.C. until l620 A.D. when the Pilgrims wrote and signed *The Mayflower Compact,* history had proved God's words to be true. This action on the part of Israel began the "divine right of kings" theory of government which gave man the "divine right" to rule over man, from which much suffering had come.

The Pilgrims had certainly learned that by hard experience!

They knew from the scriptures that God had spoken directly to the nation Israel through His prophets and judges, but they also knew he was directing *them* by speaking to their hearts and minds as individual Christians through His Living Word, Jesus, and written Word, *The Bible,* and through circumstances.

As they studied the scriptures, they were gaining an understanding of the importance of each individual in God's sight, and catching a vision of what government might be "...when governor and governed agreed to bow to the sovereignty of God."[3]

They were grasping the fact that all laws--civil and ecclesiastical--were subject to God's Law of Liberty: "But who looketh into the perfect law of liberty and continueth therein, he being not a forgetful hearer, but a doer of the word, is blessed indeed."[4]

Thus the Pilgrim with his open *Bible,* subject to the Word of God and to Christ his King, became the pioneer of America's form of civil government--a Christian republic whose representatives were godly men elected to protect the people.

To the Pilgrims, *The Bible* was the means of an individual's salvation and the means of reforming his life-- his relation not only to God but to his neighbor. It became the basis for reforming not only church government but also civil government and was their political textbook for establishing, maintaining, and protecting Christian civil government. The reason it is still used to swear in witnesses in our courts and our elected leaders into office is because, as the Pilgrims and leaders of the Reformation proclaimed, *Sola Scriptura--The Bible alone is the measure of truth.*[5]

Following is the complete *Mayflower Compact:* (The underlining is mine. It indicates the words which were omitted from the current (1985) 11th grade standard textbook in use in my city and state, and around the land--*Rise of the American Nation,* by Harcourt Brace Jovanovich, Heritage Edition. Please note that this textbook, like too many other textbooks today, has cut out the compact with God and each other, thus depriving our school children of the knowledge of the purpose for which the Pilgrims came and the heritage they paid so great a price to give to us.)*

THE MAYFLOWER COMPACT

"In ye name of God, Amen. We whose names are underwritten,

the loyal subjects of our dread soveraigne Lord, King James, by ye grace of God, of Great Britaine, France, and Ireland king, defender of the faith, & c., having undertaken, for ye glorie of God, and advancements of ye Christian faith, and honour of our king & countrie, a voyage to plant ye first colonie in ye Northerne parts of Virginia, do by these presents solemnly & mutually in ye presence of God and one another, covenant & combine ourselves togeather into a civil body politick, for our better ordering & preservation & furtherance of ye ends aforesaid; and by vertue hereof to enacte, constitute, and frame such just & equal laws, ordinances, acts, constitutions & offices, from time to time, as shall be thought most meete & convenient for ye general good of ye Colonie, unto which we promise all due submission and obedience. In witnes whereof we have hereunder subscribed our names at Cap-Codd ye 11 of November, in ye year of ye raigne of our soveraigne Lord, King James, of England, France, & Ireland ye eighteenth, and of Scotland ye fietie fourth. Ano. Dom.1620"[6]

After signing this historic document, they elected John Carver, "...a man godly and well approved amongst them...," to be their Governor for the following year.

They then sent 16 men ahead to gather firewood, for it was a bitterly cold November day. These men also found an abandoned cache of buried corn in a large iron pot--their first introduction to the food that was to save their lives, which reminded Bradford of the Israelites, sent ahead into the Promised Land, who returned with the first fruit.[7]

He wrote, "Being thus arrived in a good harbour and brought safe to land, they fell on their knees and blessed the God of Heaven who had brought them over the vast and furious ocean and delivered them from all the perils and miseries thereof."[8]

They had begun their venture on their knees at the dock in Holland asking God to bless their enterprise. They began their sojourn in America again on their knees on the cold unfriendly shore at Cape Cod, thanking God for answering their prayers.

Having searched the scripture for God's will for them and their children, they were convinced He had brought them into this new land to found a Christian nation which would be a light to the whole world. They were convinced God had a specific "call" on this country and the people who were to inhabit it, and that this call was to be worked out in terms of their covenant with Him and each other in direct continuation of the covenant promise of God to Abraham, "...in thee shall all the nations of the earth be blessed."[9]

Their diaries and letters contained many stories of God's "wonder-working providence in their lives." They had no doubt that God did keep His end of His covenant not only on an individual, but also on a corporate basis. Their concern was that *they* should keep *their* covenant with Him.

Having read in *The Bible* of the unhappy experiences of the Israelites in the wilderness whose complaints kept them from The Promised Land, the Pilgrims were careful not to murmur or complain when things went wrong. Instead they sought where *they* had gone wrong as individuals and as a people and repented, claiming the promise of God, "If my people, which are called by my name, will humble themselves and pray, seek my face, and turn from their wicked way, then will I hear from heaven, forgive their sin, and heal their land."[10]

* On March 4, 1987, as this book was going to press, Chief Judge W. C. Hand of the U.S. District Court for Alabama ruled that this and 37 other humanistic books could no longer be furnished or used as textbooks in the schools of Alabama!

Landing of the Pilgrims, 1620, by Enrico Causici, Rotunda above East door

CHAPTER FOUR

Why Did These Pilgrims Suffer So?

The Pilgrims were greeted in the new land by a barrage of arrows from hostile Indians. "Yet by the especial providence of God, none of their arrows hit or hurt us...," recorded William Bradford, "so, after we had given God thanks for our deliverance...we went on our journey and called this place 'The first encounter.'"[1]

This encounter with the Indians occurred three weeks after they arrived in America. They had assembled a longboat which ten of the Pilgrims and some seaman boarded "...intending to circulate that deep bay of Cape Cod." They were in search of a harbour one of the sailors knew of where they could build their colony. During the second night they were awakened by blood-curdling yells. The next morning, after prayer and breakfast, the cry went up, "Indians, Indians!" and "...withal, arrows came flying in amongst them...The cry of the Indians was dreadful..." Finally several of the Pilgrims in coats of mail fired their guns and the Indians scattered without any casualties on either side.

Soon after this narrow escape the frozen weather turned to blinding snow and rough seas broke their rudder and their mast, almost wrecking them. By rowing frantically they landed after having narrowly escaped crashing on a cove full of breakers.

Awaking to sunshine after a wet, cold, miserable night, they observed the sabbath. The next day they discovered the storm had taken them past the harbour they had been seeking and brought them to a little island in the middle of a perfect natural harbour deep enough to take ships twice the draft of the *Mayflower*.

The soil across on the mainland was well-drained and fertile with an open field to defend it and four spring-fed creeks of delicious pure water. Wonder of wonders, twenty acres of ground had already been cleared and was ready to plant--which, in their weakened condition, could mean the difference between life and death.

They named it Plimouth for the last town they had left in England because they had experienced such kindness from some Christians there.

Realizing they desperately needed his ship's shelter, they hastened to return to the *Mayflower* to persuade Captain Smith to remain for the winter. Having been won by their bravery, cheerfulness, and lack of complaint, he readily consented. His heart might have been softened because, while they were away, William Bradford's wife had gone overboard and drowned. (He never mentioned this tragedy in his writings and it was recorded only briefly in their other records, which has led to speculation that she might have taken her own life.)

Faced with the choice of bitterness or impotence...or getting on with establishing a colony in this wilderness, we should be thankful Bradford chose the latter because in a few months Governor Carver died and he was elected Governor. It was the courage and wisdom of this mature thirty-year-old that saved the colony from the tragic end of the Jamestown Colony.

Soon after the landing of the Pilgrims the terrible "General Sickness" fell upon them. Weak from months at sea, they began to succumb to scurvy and colds which turned into pneumonia or consumption because there had been too much work to do to rest. A half dozen died in December and eight in January. At one time there were only five men well enough to care for the rest.

On January 14 the thatched roof of the common house where the sick were being cared for by the few still on their feet suddenly caught fire.

"Had it not been for the supernatural strength given to some of the ill to take speedy action, they might all have been blown to pieces, for there were open barrels of gunpowder and loaded muskets stored there. Fortunately, the timbers in the roof did not catch fire, so the building was saved. Much precious clothing was burned up, however, further exposing them to the bitter cold of the New England winter."

"In these hard and difficult beginnings they found some discontents & murmurings arise amongst some and mutinous speeches...but they were soon quelled & overcome by ye wisdome, patience, and just & equall carrage of things by ye Govr..." (who also was among the ill.)

"But what was most sadd & lamentable was, that in 2 or 3 months time half of their company dyed, espetialy in Jan: and February, being ye depth of winter...of l00 & odd persons, scarce 50. remained. And in these times of most distres, there was but 6. or 7. sound persons whom, to their great comendations be it spoken, spaired no pains, night nor day, but with abundance of toyle and hazard of their owne health, fetched them woode, made them fires, drest them meat, made their beads, washed their lothsome cloaths, cloathed & uncloathed them, in a word, did all ye homly & necessarie offices for them which dainty & quesi stomachs cannot endure to hear named; and all this willingly & cherfully, without any grudging in ye least, shewing here their true love unto their friends & brethren...

"And all this while ye Indians came skulking about them..."[2]

But, compared to the Jamestown colony in Virginia which lost 80 to 90 percent before it was abandoned--although landing in a warm season and a warmer climate--the Pilgrims realized they had fared remarkably well.

Retaining their thankful spirit, they reminded each other that their dead were in heaven, which the Pilgrims regarded as their true home, and that they who had been spared were in the hands of a loving God who had important work for them to do.

Between the greed and perfidy of the Adventurers who for many years collected exorbitant amounts from the Pilgrims, taking advantage of their desire that their witness be not spoiled by debts, and the many who soon came without the commitment of the Pilgrims, their trials became so many their governor wrote in l647 explaining why these Christians suffered so:

"...one reason may be, that ye Divell may carrie a greater spite against ye churches of Christ and ye gospell hear, by how much ye more they endeavour to preserve holynes and puritie amongst them, and strictly punisheth the contrary when it ariseth either in church or comone wealth; ...But it may be demanded how came it to pass that so many wicked persons and profane people should so quickly come over into this land & mixe them selves amongst them? seeing it was religious men yt began ye work, and they came for religions sake. I confess this may be marveilled at, at least in time to come, when the reasons thereof should not be knowne; and ye more because here was so many hardships and wants mett withall. I shall endeavor to give some answer hereunto. And first, according to yt in ye gospell, it is ever to be remembered that wher ye Lord begins to sow good seed, ther ye envious man will endeavore to sow tares...Againe, the Lord's blesing usually following his people, as well in outward as spirituall things (though afflictions be mixed withall,) do make many to adhear to ye people of God, as many followed Christ, for ye loaves sake, John 6.26. and a mixed multitude came into ye wildernes with ye people of God out of Eagipte of old, Exod. 12. 38; so allso ther were sente by their freinds some under hope yt they would be made better; others that they might be eased of such burthens, and they kept from shame at home yt one means or other, in 20 years time, it is a question whether ye greater part be not growne ye worser..."[3]

But none of the Pilgrims returned to England and everyone of them was convinced that it was all worth the price.

Their Governor and historian continued, "...ye marvelous providence of God, that notwithstanding ye many changes and hardships that these people wente through, and ye many enemies they had and difficulties they mette with all, that so many of them should live to a very olde age!...What was it then that upheld them? It was Gods vissitation that preserved their spirits. Job 10.12. Thou has gived me life and grace, and thy vissitation hath preserved my spirite. He that upheld ye Apostle upheld them. They were persecuted, but not forsaken, cast downe, but perished not. 2 Cor: 4. 9. As unknowen, and yet knowen; as dying, and behold we live; as chastened, and yett not kiled. 2. Cor: 6. 9. God, it seems, would have all men to behold and observe such mercies and works of his providence as these are towards his people, that they in like case might be encouraged to depend upon God in their trials, & also blese his name when they see his goodnes towards others. Man lives not by bread only, Deut: 8.3. It is not by goode & dainty fare, by peace, & rest, and harts ease, in enjoying ye contentments and good things of this world only, that preserves health and prolongs life. God in such examples would have ye world see & behold that he can doe it without them; and if ye world will shut ther eyes and take no notice therof, yet he would have his people to see and consider it."[4]

So, as the First Century Church they sought to emulate suffered, these Pilgrims also endured great trials and tribulations. But they brought forth the most blessed nation the world has ever known. History shows our Christian freedoms have never come cheaply and never will, for what is of great value carries a great price!

The First Sermon Ashore, J.L.G. Ferris, Archives of 76, Bay Village, Ohio

CHAPTER FIVE

Why Were The Pilgrims
So Thankful?

The turning point in the Pilgrims' fortune occurred about the middle of March when Samoset, an Indian Chief of the Algonquin tribe appeared in the settlement and greeted them with the English word, "Welcome!"

Telling them they had settled in the only place where they were safe from hostile Indians, he explained that this area had always been the territory of the Patuxets--a large hostile tribe who had brutally murdered every white man who landed on their shores. According to Samoset, four years before the Pilgrims arrived a mysterious plague had killed every one of the Patuxets. Neighboring tribes, convinced some great supernatural spirit had destroyed them, would not come near the place.

This explained why the land had been already prepared for planting and why the Indians had left them alone!

After spending the night, Samoset left and returned a week later with Squanto, a Patuxet, who, according to William Bradford, was "...a special instrument sent of God for their good, beyond their expectation."[1]

The amazing chain of events in Squanto's life reminded the Pilgrims of the Biblical story of Joseph whose brothers sold him into slavery. When famine came in Egypt he was used by God to save his people and many others from starvation. In the end he was able to say to them, "You meant it for evil, but God meant it for good."[2]

Captured and taken to England by Capt. George Weymouth, Squanto had been taught English so that he might be able to supply information about his homeland that would help the English to establish colonies in the best places.

After nine years, Capt. John Smith brought him back to New England where he was again captured and taken to Spain to be sold into slavery. Rescued by local friars who introduced him to the Christian faith, he soon attached himself to an Englishman bound for London. He had returned to his homeland six months before the Pilgrims arrived and found not one member of his tribe alive. Wandering and lost, with no purpose in life, he had been taken in by Massasoit, chief of the Wampanoags, whose territory was some 50 miles to the west of Plymouth Colony.

Samoset and Squanto spent the night and left, returning a few days later with Massasoit and the men of his tribe. Probably the only chief on the northeast coast who would welcome the white man as a friend, Massasoit was also a remarkable example of God's providential care of His Pilgrims.[3]

During their visit, with Squanto acting as interpreter, the Wampanoags and the Pilgrims made a treaty which remained in effect for forty years. The Pilgrims showed the Indians the love of Christ in them and were careful not to abuse their trust, and they always lived in peace and friendship with each other.

Squanto, at long last having found his reason for being, stayed to teach the Pilgrims how to fish, stalk deer and other animals, plant corn and pumpkins, refine maple syrup, know herbs and their food and medicinal purposes, where to find berries, how to hunt and trade the pelts of beavers, and hundreds of things these strangers to the wilderness needed to learn in order to survive.

By October, the Pilgrims were filled with gratitude not only to Massasoit and Squanto who had helped them so greatly, but to God who had rewarded their faith and obedience so graciously and miraculously.

Governor William Bradford declared a day of public Thanksgiving and invited Massasoit. He arrived a day early with ninety Indians. This was the greatest test of their faith as they realized their precious food might be decimated for the winter; but God was faithful as they again trusted Him. The Indians had brought five dressed deer and over a dozen fat turkeys. They helped with the cooking, teaching the Pilgrims to make hoecakes, popcorn, and pudding from cornmeal and maple syrup. In turn, the Pilgrims introduced the Indians to vegetables from their gardens--carrots, onions, turnips, parsnips, cucumbers, radishes--and blueberry, apple, and cherry pie and sweet wine made from wild grapes.[4]

The Indians had such a great time they stayed for three days. On this historic first Thanksgiving both groups learned God's law of giving: "Give and to you shall be given, good measure, pressed down, and running over."[5]

From that time on, America has been, without question, the most generous nation the world has ever known, and has prospered as no other nation.

But the problems the Pilgrims faced and the lessons they were to learn did not end with that first Thanksgiving. A year after the landing of the Pilgrims Mr. Cushman, who had caused them so much trouble in the beginning and was to continue to, arrived along with "35 persons to remaine & liv in ye planation...ther was not so much as a bisket-cake or any other victials for them, neither had they any beding, but some sory things they had in their cabins, nor pot, nor pan, to drese any meate in..."[6]

In the ship was a letter from Mr. Weston to Governor Carver who, along with his wife, had died that terrible winter. In it he complained that they had kept the Mayflower so long, and returned her empty![7]

With nearly twice as many to feed, they went on half rations. Next, seven more persons arrived from a fishing boat sent out by Mr. Weston "with no victails, nor any hope of any." In a later boat Weston sent "60. lusty men" who stayed with them for a while and then moved on, leaving their sick to be provided and cared for by the hard-pressed Pilgrims and saying they didn't want to be encumbered with women and children.[8]

"But they were an unruly company, and had no good governmente over them, and by disorder would soone fall into wants..." predicted Bradford, and he was right. They soon learned that Weston's people, who had settled in Massachusetts, were in severe want, working all day for the Indians. Bradford wrote "...in ye end, they came to that misery, that some starved and dyed with could & hunger...Yet they left all ther sicke folk hear till they were setled and housed,"

31

He concluded, "...Psa. 118.8 'It is better to trust in the Lord than to have confidence in man.' And Psa. 146,. 'Put not your trust in princes (much less in ye marchants) nor in ye sons of man, for ther is no help in them. v.5.' And as they were now fayled of suply by him (Weston) and others in this their greatest neede and wants, which was caused by him and ye rest who put so great a company of men upon them, as ye former company were, without any food, and came at such a time as they must live almost a whole year before any could be raised, excepte they had sente some; so, upon ye pointe they never had any supply of victails more afterwards (but what the Lord gave them otherwise); for all ye company sent at any time was always too short for those people yt came with it...

"Thus all ther hopes in regard of Mr. Weston were layed in ye dust, and all his promised helpe turned into an empttie advice, which they apprehended was nether lawfull nor profitable for them to follow."[9]

Bradford wrote, "...when famine begane now to pinch them sore, they not knowing what to doe, turned to the Lord, (who never fails his,)..." and that they were given help "...beyond all expectation. This boat which came from ye eastward brought them a letter from a stranger, of whose name they had never heard before, being a captaine of a ship come ther a fishing...Whereupon they sent Mr. Winslow in a boat...to procure what provissions he could of ye ships, who was kindly received by ye aforesaid gentill-man, who not only spared what he could, but writ to others to doe ye like."[10]

Divided among so many, it wasn't much, but, aided by another ship which had a store of beads and knives they were able to trade with the Indians for corn and survive until harvest time.[11]

Not one of them starved that winter of 1621-22, although they were ultimately reduced to a daily ration of five kernels of corn! On future Thanksgiving Days, they put 5 kernels of corn on their plates to remind themselves of where they had come from.

In order to obtain passage to America, the Pilgrims had agreed to communal farming and indentured themselves to the "London

Adventurers" for seven years, but it was becoming apparent they must act, or meet the same fate that had destroyed Jamestown. It was clearly a matter of life or death.

"...after much debate of things, Governor Bradford (with the advice of the chiefest amongst them) gave way that they should set corn every man for his own particular, and in that regard trust to themselves." The single men were assigned to families, and every family was assigned a parcel of land according to the proportion of their number.

"This had very good success; for it made all hands very industrious," reported Bradford, adding, "the experience that was had in this comone course and condition tried sundrie years, and that among godly and sober men, may well evince the vanitie of that conceite of Platos & other ancients, applauded by some of later times; - that ye taking away propertie, and bringing in comunitie into a comone wealth, would make them happy and florishing; as if they were wiser than God...God in his wisdome saw another course fiter for them."[12]

The free enterprise system and the "American Work Ethic" which has benefited Americans and all who followed it was introduced into the Pilgrim colony on the basis of the scripture, "But if any provide not for his own, and specially for those of his own house, he hath denied the faith, and is worse than an infidel."[13]

Bradford wrote that when this was begun, "...all ther victails were spent, and they were only to rest on God's providence; at night not many times knowing where to have a bit of any thing ye next day. And so, as one well observed, had need to pray that God would give them their dayly brade, above all people in ye world."[14]

Not only did the Pilgrims receive letters from the "Adventurers" by which they heard of "their furder crosses and frustrations," but they experienced "...a great drought which continued from ye 3. weeke in May til bout ye midle of July, without any raine, and with great heat (for ye most parte), insomuch as ye corn begane to wilter away...Upon which they set aparte a solemne day of humiliation, to seek ye Lord by humble & fervent prayer, in this great distrese."

It was God's "gracious and speedy answer, both to their own and the Indians admiration, that lived amongst them," that led to their second Thanksgiving celebration.

All that morning it was clear and very hot, not a cloud in sight. "...yet toward evening it begane to overcast, and shortly after to raine, with such sweete and gentle showers as gave them cause of rejoyceing blesing God. It came without either wind, or thunder, or any violence, and by degreese of yt abundance, as that ye earth was thoroughly wete and soked therewith...afterwards the Lord sent them such seasonable showers, with enterchange of faire warm weather, as, through his blessing, caused a fruitfull & liberal harvest...For which mercie (in time conveniente;) they also sett apart a day of thanksgiving."[15]

Their historian reported that while 60 more ill-prepared people arrived, they must pay for what they needed. "By this time harvest was come, and instead of famine, now God gave them plentie, and ye face of things was changed, to ye rejoyceing of ye harts of many, for which they blessed God...so as any general wante or famine hath not been amongst them since to this day..."[16]

The Return of the Mayflower, J.L.T. Ferris, Archives of 76, Bay Village, Ohio

CHAPTER SIX

What Have These Pilgrims To Do With Us?

Half of the people who came over on the Mayflower died of disease, exposure, and malnutrition that first winter, but not one of them went back with the crew.[1]

Although they could not know the ultimate significance of their endurance and perseverance, a later historian wrote, "There is importance in every event which in any degree affected the question whether the settlement should be maintained or abandoned; for reading between the lines of that question there is seen within it another, as to whether posterity should behold an Anglo-Saxon state on the American continent. Had Plymouth been deserted by the Pilgrim Fathers in 1621-22, Massachusetts Bay would have remained desolate, and even Virginia would doubtless have been abandoned. Then, before new colonization could be organized, France would have made good her claim by pushing down our Atlantic coast until she met Spain ascending from the south--unless, indeed, Holland had retained her hold at the center...Such were some of the momentous issues that were largely decided by the apparently little things which make up the Pilgrim history...

"Sir Thomas Hutchinson, whose tastes would not have led him to an undue estimation of the uncourtly and unchartered settlers at Plymouth, thus spoke of them in his History:

"'These were the founders of the Colony at New Plymouth. The settlement of this Colony occasioned the settlement of Massachusetts Bay, which was the source of all the other Colonies in New England. Virginia was in a dying state, and seemed to revive and flourish from the example of New England.'"[2]

36

Our Great Seal, which was adopted in 1782, must surely have had its roots in Plymouth Plantation, for who contributed more to the beginning of this nation, and who understood better than the Pilgrims its inscription, *Novus Ordo Seclorum*--A New Order Is Begun? Or believed more firmly *Annuit Coeptis*--He Has Favored Our Undertaking or, as the young lady who applies the Great Seal on official documents in the State Department translated it, "He has smiled on our enterprise?"

Who understood better than those who called themselves "stepping-stones" that the building of this nation is far from complete, as is the pyramid on the Great Seal? Who was more aware of the eye of God overlooking its building? Who understood better than they the symbolism of the rings of light around the thirteen stars representing the religious enlightenment of our nation's founders.[3]

The Pilgrim historian and governor, William Bradford, wrote, "As one candle may light a thousand, so the light kindled here has shown unto many, yea in some sort to our whole nation...We have noted these things so that you might see their worth and not negligently lose what your fathers have obtained with so much hardship."[4]

And who understood our motto, *In God We Trust,* on every one of our coins and bills, more than they? And, like Chaucer's Poor Parson, first lived by it more?[5]

"We should never forget that the prison, the scaffold, and the stake were stages in the march of civil and religious liberty which our forefathers had to travel, in order that we might attain our present liberty," wrote John Overton Choules. "Before our children remove their religious connections...before they leave the old paths of God's Word...before they barter their birthright for a mess of pottage - let us place in their hands this chronicle of the glorious days of the suffering Churches, and let them know that they are the sons of the men of whom the world was not worthy, and whose sufferings for conscience' sake are here monumentally recorded."[6]

"Fleeing both ecclesiastical and civil tyranny, the valiant Pilgrims of Plymouth Plantation brought to these shores Primitive Christianity. Like their counterpart of the first century, they witnessed by their lives the consistency of their faith.

37

"In the record of Plymouth Colony can be found the seed of all our important institutions. Here begins our precious heritage of Christian Character, Christian Self-Government, Christian Economics, Christian Education, and Biblical Christian Unity. For it is what constitutes the character of individual Americans that determines whether our government, economics, education, and unity are Christian or pagan," wrote Rosalie Slater, who spent twenty-five years studying in the archives of America.[7]

One of the first acts of George Washington after assuming the presidency was to issue the following Thanksgiving Proclamation:

"Whereas, it is the duty of all nations to acknowledge the Providence of Almighty God, to obey his will, to be grateful for his benefits, and humbly to implore his protection and favor; and, whereas, both Houses of Congress have, by their joint committee, requested me to recommend to the people of the United States a day of public thanksgiving and prayer, to be observed by acknowledging with grateful hearts the many and signal favors of Almighty God, especially by affording them an opportunity peaceably to establish a form of government for their safety and happiness;

"Now, therefore, I do recommend and assign Thursday, the twenty-sixth day of November next, to be devoted by people of these States to the service of that great and glorious Being, who is the beneficent Author of all the good that was, that is, or that will be; that we may then all unite in rendering to Him our sincere and humble thanks for his kind care and protection of the people of this country, previous to their becoming a nation, for the signal and manifold mercies, and the favorable interpositions of His providence, in the course and conclusion of the late war; for the great degree of tranquillity, union, and plenty, which we have since enjoyed; for the peaceable and rational manner in which we have been enabled to establish constitutions of government for our safety and happiness, and particularly the national one now lately instituted; for the civil and religious liberty with which we are blessed, and the means we have of acquiring and diffusing useful knowledge; and, in general, for all the great and various favors, which He has been pleased to confer upon us.

"And, also, that we may then unite in most humbly offering our prayers and supplications to the great Lord and Ruler of

Nations, and beseech Him to pardon our national and other transgressions; to enable us all, whether in public or private stations, to perform our several and relative duties properly and punctually; to render our national government a blessing to all the people, by constantly being a government of wise, just, and constitutional laws, discreetly and faithfully executed and obeyed; to protect and guide all sovereigns and nations (especially such as have shown kindness to us), and to bless them with good governments, peace, and concord; to promote the knowledge and practice of true religion and virtue, and the increase of science, among them and us; and generally to grant unto all mankind such a degree of temporal prosperity as He alone knows to be best.

"Given under my hand, at the city of New York, the third day of October, in the year of our Lord one thousand seven hundred and eighty-nine." [8]

On the bicentennial of the landing of the Pilgrims, Daniel Webster spoke at Plymouth, calling it "...the spot where the first scene of our history was laid; where the hearths and altars of New England were first placed; where Christianity, and civilization, and letters made their first lodgement, in a vast extent of country, covered with a wilderness, and peopled by roving barbarians...

"Cultivated mind was to act on uncultivated nature; and more than all, a government and a country were to commence, with the very first foundations laid under the divine light of the Christian religion. Happy auspices of a happy futurity! Who would wish that his country's existence had otherwise begun?. ..Who would wish for other emblazoning of his country's heraldry, or other ornaments of her genealogy, than to be able to say, that her first existence was with intelligence, her first breath the inspiration of liberty, her first principle the truth of divine religion?...

"...We hold these institutions of government, religion, and learning, to be transmitted as well as enjoyed. We are in the line of conveyance, through which whatever has been obtained by the spirit and efforts of our ancestors is to be communicated to our children...

"We are bound to maintain public liberty, and, by the example of our own systems, to convince the world that order and law,

39

religion and morality, the rights of conscience, the rights of persons, and the rights of property, may all be preserved and secured, in the most perfect manner, by a government entirely and purely elective. If we fail in this, our disaster will be signal, and will furnish an argument, stronger than has yet been found, in support of those opinions which maintain that government can rest safely on nothing but power and coercion...

"Finally, let us not forget the religious character of our origin. Our fathers were brought hither by their high veneration for the Christian religion. They journeyed by its light, and labored in its hope. They sought to incorporate its principles with the elements of their society, and to diffuse its influence through all their institutions, civil, political, or literary. Let us cherish these sentiments, and extend this influence still more widely; in the full conviction, that that is the happiest society which partakes in the highest degree of the mild and peaceful spirit of Christianity."[9]

Throughout the years there were sporadic celebrations of Thanksgiving until Sarah Jesoha Hale, editor of *Ladies Magazine,* began a one-woman crusade to have Thanksgiving celebrated annually as a national holiday. In 1863, after her last Thanksgiving editorial, President Lincoln issued a Proclamation making Thanksgiving an official annual national holiday, which it remains to this day--one of the three early American holidays unique to America and celebrated by every state.

Declaration of Independence in Congress, by John Trumbull, Capitol Rotunda

Monument for the Battle of Lexington

The Fourth of July--
The Birth of a Nation

CHAPTER ONE

At Long Last, The Birth of a Christian Nation!

On July 4, 1776, fifty-six courageous American colonists signed the birth certificate of the United States of America, The Declaration of Independence. The first nation to emerge as a Christian nation was ushered in with the greatest document to ever flow from the hand of man alone.

In a burst of enthusiasm, John Adams wrote his wife, Abigail, "It is the will of heaven that the two countries should be sundered forever..."[1]

Samuel Adams, who was called "The Father of the American Revolution," wrote, "The people, I am told, recognize the resolution as though it were a decree promulgated from heaven."[2]

Close to a century later, Abraham Lincoln (under the stress of a war incited by a Supreme Court decision in the Dred Scott case that slaves could not vote because they were not legal citizens and had no rights) described this new nation as "...conceived in liberty and dedicated to the proposition that all men are created equal.."[3]

Did these men who laid their lives, their fortunes, and their sacred honor on the line that historic day realize the ultimate significance of what they had brought forth?

After ten years of frustration, we might think they were more concerned with the immediate consequences of what they had just done than the ultimate impact on the human race. After all, they were only three million people on the edge of a wilderness who had very recently been fighting for their existence in a war with the French and Indians. Now they were up against the strongest nation in the world, their own motherland, from whose oppression some of them and many of their ancestors had fled to America. How could they know this nation they were founding would become the strongest, most blessed nation in the history of the world? Or that it would draw freedom lovers not just from Europe but from every part of the earth?

And yet one of the signers of the Declaration of Independence, John Adams, wrote his wife, "Yesterday, the greatest question was decided that was ever debated in America, and greater, perhaps, never was or will be decided among men. A resolution was passed, without one dissenting colony, 'that these United colonies are, and of right ought to be, free and independent states.'"[4]

Almost all of them were deeply committed to the Christian faith for which they or their ancestors had suffered severe affliction in England, Ireland, Scotland, Germany, Holland and France. Almost all of them believed the promise of Jesus, "If the Son therefore shall set you free, ye shall be free indeed."[5]

Many of their ancestors, believing this, had brought forth the thirteen colonies the Second Continental Congress represented with the following documents:

First Charter for Colonizing Virginia, April 10/20, 1606

"...III.--We greatly commending and graciously accepting of their Desires for so noble a Work, which may, by the Providence of Almighty God, hereafter tend to the Glory of his Divine Majesty, in propagating of Christian Religion to such people as yet live in Darkness and miserable Ignorance of the true knowledge and Worship of God..."

The Mayflower Compact (November 11/21, 1620

"In the name of God, Amen...haveing undertaken, for the glorie of God; and advancement of the Christian faith...do by these presents solemnly and mutually in the presence of God, and one of another, covenant and combine ourselves together into a civil body politick, for the better ordering and preservation and furtherance of the ends aforesaid..."

The Fundamental Orders of 1639--Conn. Colonial Records 1, 20-25

"Foreasmuch as it hath pleased the Almighty God by the wise disposition of his divine providence so to Order and dispose of things...And well knowing where a people are gathered together the word of God requires that to mayntayne the peace and union of such a people there should be an orderly and decent Government established according to God...to mayntayne and presearve the liberty and purity of the gospel of our Lord Jesus which we now professe, as also the disciplyne of the Churches, which according to the truth of the said gospell is now practised amongst us:..."

The New England Confederation Constitution--Plymouth Colony Records IX, betwixt the Plantations under the government of Massachusetts...the Government of Plimouth...of Connecticut...of New Haven, (1663)

"Whereas we all came into these parts of America, with one and the same end and ayme, namely, to advance the Kingdome of our Lord Jesus Christ, and to enjoy the liberties of the Gospel, in purity with peace; and whereas in our settling (by a wise providence of God) we are further dispersed upon the Sea-Coast, and Rivers, than was at first intended..."

Penn's Charter of Privileges of Pennsylvania, Oct. 28/Nov.8, 1701 (Vote and proceeding of the House of Representatives of Pennsylvania, I, pt.II, i-iii)

"1. Because no People can be truly happy, tho' under the greatest Enjoyment of civil Liberties, if abridged of the freedom of Conscience, as to their Religious Profession and Worship; and Almighty God being the only Lord of Conscience, Father of Lights and Spirits; and the Author as well as the Object of all divine Knowledge, Faith, and Worship, who only doth enlighten the Minds, and persuade and convince the Understandings of People, I do hereby grant and declare, That no Person or Persons, inhabiting in this Province or Territories, who shall confess and acknowledge One Almighty God, the Creator, upholder and ruler of the World...shall be in any Case molested or prejudiced, in his or their Person or Estate, because of his or their conscientious Persuasion or Practice...And that all Persons who also profess to believe in Jesus Christ, the Saviour of the World, shall be capable (nothwithstanding their other Persuasions and Practices in point of Conscience and Religion) to serve this Government in any Capacity...

The Rhode Island Charter, (Rhode Island Colonial Records, II, 3-20), 1644

"...they, pursueing, with peaceable and loyall minds, their sober, serious and religious intentions, of godlie edifieing themselves, and one another, in the holie Christian faith and worshipp as they were persuaded; together with the gaineing over and conversione of the poore ignorant Indian natives, in those parts of America, to the sincere professione and obedience of the same faith and worship, did, not only by the consent and good encouragement of our royal progenitors, transport themselves out of this kingdome of England into America,...where by the good Providence of God, from whome the Plantationes have taken their name (Providence, R.I.)...have freely declared that it is much on their hearts (if they may be permitted) to hold forth a livelie experiment, that a most flourishing civill state may stand and best be maintained, and that among our English subjects, with a full libertie in religious concernments; and that true pietye rightly grounded upon gospell principles, will give the best and greatest security to sovereignetye, and will lay in the hearts of men the strongest obligations of true loyaltie...to secure them in the free exercise and enjoyment of all theire civill and religious rights...and to preserve them that libertie, in the true Christian faith and worshipp of God, which they have sought with soe much travaill..."

Maryland Toleration Act of 1649 (Maryland Archives I, 244 ff.)

"Foreasmuch as in a well-governed and Christian Common Wealth, matters concerning Religion and the honor of God ought in the first place to be taken into serious consideration...be it therefore ordered and enacted...that whatsoer person or persons within this Province and the Islands thereunto belonging shall from henceforth blaspheme God...or deny the Holy Trinity, the Father, Sonne and Holy Ghost...or shall use...any reproachful Speeches...concerning the said Holy Trinity, or any of the three persons thereof, shall be punished with death and confiscation of all his or her lands and goods ...no person or persons whatsoever within this Province...professing to believe in Jesus Christ, shall from henceforth be any waies troubled, Molested or discountenanced for or in respect of his or her religion nor in the free exercise thereof...nor any way compelled to the beleife or exercise of any other Religion against his or her consent...that all and every person; and persons that shall presume Contrary to this Act and the true intent and meaning there of directly, or indirectly either in person or estate wilfully to wrong disturbe trouble or molest any person whatsoever within this Province professing to believe in Jesus Christ for or in respect to his religion or the free exercise thereof within this Province...that such person or persons soe offending shall be compelled to pay trebble damage to the party soe wronged...(or, in default of payment, shall make satisfaction by public whipping or imprisonment during the pleasure of the Governor..."

Further evidence of how eleven of the thirteen colonies covenanted with God and each other in their charters, may be found in our national and state archives.

The founding fathers left no doubt as to the religious nature of this new nation. They clearly described it in the two opening sentences and in the two sentences that closed the Declaration of Independence:

It began, "When in the course of human events, it becomes necessary for one people to dissolve the political bands which have connected them with another and to assume, among the powers of the earth, *the separate and equal station to which the laws of nature and of nature's God entitle them,* a decent respect to the opinions of mankind requires that they should declare the causes which impel them to the separation,

"We hold these truths to be self-evident, that all men are created equal; that they are endowed by their Creator with certain unalienable rights; that among these are life, liberty, and the pursuit of happiness..."

It concluded, "We, therefore, the representatives of the United States of America, in General Congress assembled, *appealing to the Supreme Judge of the World for the rectitude of our intentions,* do, in the name and by the authority of the good people of these colonies solemnly publish and declare that these United Colonies are, and of right ought to be, Free and Independent States: that they are absolved from all allegiance to the British crown, and that all political connection between them and the State of Great

Britain is, and ought to be, totally dissolved; and that as free and independent States, they have full power to levy war, conclude peace, contract alliances, establish commerce and to do all other acts and things which independent States may of right do. *And for the support of this declaration, with a firm reliance on the protection of Divine Providence, we mutually pledge to each other our lives, our fortunes, and our sacred honor.*" (Underline and italics in original document)

Thus, the signers of *The Declaration of the Independence* renewed the covenant of the signers of the *Mayflower Compact* to place their government under God. And, what is more, they did it! After nearly 3000 years of man's dominion over man, the United States was now officially under the dominion of the God of the Bible and of His Son, Jesus, to whom He gave all authority in heaven and on earth, including that of "...the Supreme Judge of the World," mentioned in the *Declaration of Independence*.[6]

Justice Lifts the Nation, Supreme Court Building, Lausanne, Switzerland

CHAPTER TWO

Where Were These Revolutionaries Coming From?

"It was Calvinism that first revealed the worth and dignity of man. Called of God, and heir of Heaven, the trader at his counter and the digger in his field suddenly rose in equality with the noble and the king," wrote Anglican historian John Richard Green.[1]

Of the estimated three million people who lived in the colonies at the time of the Revolutionary War, 900,000 were of Scotch or Scotch-Irish origin, 600,000 were Puritan English, while over 400,000 were of Dutch, German Reformed, and Huguenot descent. "That is to say," explains Dr. Egbert Watson Smith, "two-thirds of our Revolutionary forefathers were trained in the school of Calvin."[2]

Other historians agreed with him. George Bancroft said, "He who will not respect the memory of John Calvin knows nothing of American liberty...Calvinism was revolutionary; it taught as a divine revelation the natural equality of man."[3]

In his *History of the Reformation,* D'Aubigne affirms, "Calvin was the founder of the greatest of republics. The Pilgrims who left their country in the reign of James I, and, landing on the barren soil of New England, founded populous and mighty colonies, were his sons, his direct and legitimate sons; and that American nation which we have seen growing so rapidly boasts as its father the humble Reformer on the shores of Lake Leman (a famous lake in Geneva, Switzerland)."[4]

The teaching of Calvin on "... the dignity of human nature, of the rights of man, of national liberty, of social equality, can create such a resolve for the freedom of the soul...," wrote N. .S. McFetridge, "He who has this faith feels he is compassed about with everlasting love, guided by everlasting strength; his will is the tempered steel that no fire can melt, no force can break."[5]

Teaching the absolute sovereignty of God, the absolute equality of clergy and laity, and the absolute solidarity of mankind, John Calvin gave a concept of life which substituted the divine right of man for the divine right of kings, or as Rudyard Kipling expressed it,

> "The people, Lord, the people,
>
> Not thrones, not crowns, but men."

Alexis de Tocqueville compared the blatantly antireligious French Revolution to America's War of Independence: "In France I had almost always seen the spirit of religion and the spirit of freedom marching in opposite directions," wrote this French historian. "But in America I found they were intimately united and that they reigned in common over the same country."[6]

Leopole von Ranke, a German historian, gave the reason for this happy marriage between religion and human freedom: "John Calvin was the virtual founder of America."[7]

At the age of 26, John Calvin wrote a little book called *The Institutes of Christian Religion* and was forced to leave France, his homeland. En route to Germany to join the Reformation of Martin Luther, Calvin was induced by William Farel to remain in Geneva and continue the reformation he had already begun there by his *Institutes*.

"I felt as if God from Heaven had laid His mighty hand upon me to stop me in my course," explained the reluctant Calvin.[8]

He had a vision of turning Geneva, one of the roughest and most morally loose cities in a corrupt generation, into a model City of God on Earth, and, in spite of the annoyances and miseries he was subjected to, he wrote, "...the thought of deserting it never entered my mind. For I considered myself placed in that position by God, like a sentry at his post, from which it would be impiety on my part were I to move a single step."[9]

Meanwhile, across the border in France, the Huguenots were being burned at stake for their Reformed faith and there was the constant danger that Catholic forces might cross the border and snuff out Protestantism on the shores of Lake Leman.[10]

France never recovered from the ill effects of the persecution of its Protestants. It has been estimated that as many as four million were lost by flight or martyrdom, and even the rationalist historian, William E. H. Lecky, saw that the loss of the Huguenots "...prepared the way for the inevitable degradation of the national character and removed the last serious bulwark that might have broken the force of that torrent of skepticism and vice, which, a century later, laid prostrate in merited ruin both the altar and the throne"--referring, of course, to the bloody French Revolution which, unlike the American Revolution, was bathed with an anti-religious spirit that resulted in the Reign of Terror and the September massacres. As historian H. G. Wells said, "There was something inhuman even in their humanitarian zeal."[11]

Rowdy Geneva citizens resented Calvin's heavy-handed law-and-order teaching. However, it was the stand he took against the city council's decision to admit all citizens to the sacrament and to impose upon Geneva a specific liturgy, without even consulting the ministers, that caused Calvin and Farel to be banished from the city. Remembering the disaster to the church when Constantine required every Roman to become Christian, they took their stand firmly for freedom of choice as a God-given right of man.[12]

"The immoral element got control, and the moral life of the city became unspeakable." wrote Walter L. Lingle. "The Roman Catholic Church made a determined effort to overthrow Protestantism. Visitors, strangers, and refugees who had come to Geneva because John Calvin was there ceased to come. The people of Geneva began to realize that John Calvin was a great spiritual, moral, and financial asset. There was a growing sentiment for his return."

Finally the city council sent an invitation to Calvin to return to Geneva. but he politely refused. In 1541, upon the repeated invitation and urging of the city officials, he returned to a somewhat chastened city, amid a joyous welcome.

Calvin consulted the Bible for everything and he immediately began to apply biblical principles to the church--for government, doctrine, worship, discipline and life. The City Council approved of this Form of Government, and the church in Geneva became a Reformed Church.[13]

A statesman, educator, theologian, and minister of the Word of God, Calvin planted the seeds for freedoms to be enjoyed by later generations. As an educator, he organized the Geneva School system and was the father of popular education. He was known to his age as *the* theologian, and even the French skeptic and critic, Ernest Renan, wrote, "He succeeded more than all, in an age and in a country which called for reaction towards Christianity, simply because he was the most Christian man of his century."[14]

At the height of his influence in Geneva, he had drawn as many as 10,000 Bible students from all over Europe, including John Knox, a Scotch reformer who had come up against the corruption of the Catholic church.[15]

Knox had been forced to endure two years as a galley slave in a French vessel. Once it took him past the shoreline of his beloved Scotland where in the distance he could see the spire of the church in which he had once preached. He prayed, "O God, give me Scotland or I die," and his prayer was answered.[16]

It was in the galley of that French ship he learned the French that was to enable him to study under Calvin. And it was from Calvin that Knox learned Romans 8:28, "All things"--even those tortuous months of a living death as a galley slave--can "work together for good to them that love God, to them who are the called according to his purpose." It was that crash course in French aboard that slave ship that enabled John Knox to translate the Reformed theology of John Calvin into the rugged language of Scotland.

In his absence a number of Protestant and anti-French nobles in Scotland had entered into a covenant to "establish the most blessed Word of God and His congregation." They wrote Knox, then at Geneva, to return home immediately and establish a church based upon the form of government he had found in Calvin's Geneva. The Confession of Faith he submitted was adopted the following year by the Scottish parliament.[17]

The Scottish Reformation recognized that Protestantism and national independence were bound together. It produced, under the leadership of John Knox, one of the most remarkable documents of that age, *The Book of Discipline*, which established a code of conduct for a people that were once known to be about as unruly as any in Europe. It provided for the government of the church by sessions, synods, and the General Assembly, established a school for teaching Latin, grammar, and the catechism, and provided high school and college training for every lad capable of such study. Thus the groundwork was laid both in Geneva and Edinburgh for what was to become a hallmark of Protestant faith and life in America, an educated ministry and an equally educated laity.[18]

Immersed in the Scripture, they resisted both prelate and crown in the firm belief that "...the entrance of thy words giveth light; it giveth understanding unto the simple," and "...ye shall know the truth, and the truth shall make you free."[19]

"Knox made Calvinism the religion of Scotland, and Calvinism made Scotland the moral standard for the world," wrote Egbert Watson Smith.[20]

Believing religion should dominate every area of the lives of both men and nations, they would have nothing to do with the heresy that religion and politics don't mix. John Knox himself plunged into the rough and tumble of politics. Standing by his open grave in 1572, Regent Morton said, "Here lies one who never feared the face of man."[21]

The reformers had learned that, while scholars might sometimes debate the more obtuse points of theology, the man in the street just wants to hear the simple message of God's redeeming love in Christ. And so not only Scotland, but also England and the colonists in America became the people of a book, and that book was *The Bible.*

When the son of Mary Queen of Scots, James I, came to the throne of England and Scotland, he swore, "I will make them conform, or I will harry them out of the land or worse."[22]

"He did harry some of them out of the land," says Walter Lingle. "They came to Plymouth Rock and New England, and thus enriched the spiritual life of America. But James never succeeded in his efforts to make them conform. When he forcibly deported many to Ulster, a great revival broke out there. A great migration from the Scottish lowlands settled in northern Ireland, and they were stronger at his death than they were at the beginning of his reign."[23]

The Restoration of the monarchy under Charles II and "The Great Ejectment" of Calvinism caused the beleaguered Calvinists of Scotland, Ireland, and England to come to the New Promised Land of America. It has been conservatively estimated that between 1705 and 1775, at least one-half million fled persecution in Ulster and settled in the colonies, not counting the Scotch-Irish from northern Ireland, and the ones who came directly from Scotland.[24]

From 1660 to 1760 the number of colonists rose from 75,000 to nearly 1,600,000, so these persecuted Calvinists and their descendants comprised a large proportion of the population. As in Ireland, revival broke out soon after their coming.

The number of churches in America had increased from 154 in 1660 to 1176 in 1740 after the "Great Awakening." By 1780, four years after the Declaration of Independence, the total number of churches had increased to 2731. Of these, 56 were Roman Catholics, 495 were Presbyterian, 178 were Lutheran, 201 were German Reformed, 127 were Dutch Reformed, 749 were Congregational (which included Pilgrims and Puritans), 457 were Baptist, and 406 were Anglican. Puritans made up 600,000 of the colonials of English descent, while over 400,000 were of Dutch, German Reformed, and Huguenot descent.

Of the approximately three million colonials at the time of the Declaration of Independence, 900,000 were of Scotch or Scotch-Irish origin. (There was not a drop of Irish blood in their veins, but they were so-called because they were Scotsmen living in Ireland, having fled persecution because of their faith.)[25]

Reporting on the revolt of the colonies to the British House of Commons, Horace Walpole said, "There is no good crying about the matter. Cousin America has run off with a Presbyterian parson, and that is the end of it."[26]

He was referring to Dr. John Witherspoon, a lineal descendant of Scotland's fiery preacher-patriot John Knox, who had said to a wavering Continental Congress, "There is a tide in the affairs of men. We perceive it now before us. To hesitate is to consent to our own slavery. That noble instrument (The Declaration of

Independence) should be subscribed this very morning by every pen in this house."[27]

Could there be any doubt that the United States had its roots in Calvinism, and was an offspring of the Reformation?

Liberty's Pulpit, J.T.L. Ferris, Archives of 76, Bay Village, Ohio

CHAPTER THREE

What Was The Revolution All About?

Freedom was what it was all about.

In 1682, warned that the ministers of Massachusetts were preaching freedom, King Charles II demanded a return of that colony's charter. His edict was never carried out, but later James II ordered all the charters of the Colonies to be revoked. The Charters were again saved, this time by the overthrow of James II in the "Glorious Revolution" of William and Mary.

The colonists' rights as freeborn Englishmen were restored, bringing peace until "The Great Awakening," when again freedom became the subject of sermons throughout the colonies. Changing the traditional conceptions of social authority, it "...paved the way for emerging democratic ideals which would triumph in the American Revolution... Considered as a great social event, the Great Awakening signified nothing less than the first stage of the American Revolution."[1]

This movement of the Spirit which preceded the confrontation with Great Britain began in 1734 in Northampton, Massachusetts, in the parish of Jonathan Edwards, America's most respected and brilliant theologian. Concerned about the licentiousness of young people and troubled about the spread of spiritual self-reliance, he first visited the youths in their homes. Then he followed with a series of sermons on justification by faith alone. Preaching against the popular humanist notion that man, by his own efforts, can do anything of value, he affirmed the Reformation doctrine that man must rely totally on God's grace.

Revival began to break out in colonies hungry to reestablish their former covenant relation with God and sick of having become a people described in The Bible, II Timothy 3:5, as "...having a form of godliness, but denying the power thereof." In his *Narrative of Surprising Conversions* Jonathan Edwards reported how "...souls did, as it were, come by flocks to Jesus Christ...so that in the spring and summer following, Anno 1735, the town seemed to be full of joy...there were remarkable tokens of God's presence in almost every house. It was a time of joy in families on account of salvation's being brought unto them, parents rejoicing over their children as new born, and husbands over their wives, and wives over their husbands."[2]

He attacked head-on the liberal argument that salvation was only a life lived in reasonable accord with Christ's ethical teachings and insisted that human sin was inherent enmity and rebellion against God. He said salvation meant a radical conversion of the heart to total dependence upon the absolute sovereignty of God and stressed that unless the heart is affected through regenerative grace, religion is nothing more than rational speculation.

Thus he embraced the Reformation doctrine of "justification by faith alone," warning, "...it is none of our excellency, virtue, or righteousness that is the ground of our being received from a state of condemnation into a state of acceptance in God's sight, but only Jesus Christ, and His righteousness and worthiness, received by faith."

His most famous sermon, and perhaps the most famous sermon in American history, was "Sinners in the Hands of an Angry God." It was pure Calvanistic doctrine, and brought the American colonists in droves to repentance and a spiritual awakening.[3]

George Whitfield, a young Englishman, came to America in 1736 and by his preaching united Americans into one body--the Body of Christ. Through his preaching he overcame all the old ecclesiastical barriers. By 1770, he had preached a phenomenal eighteen thousand sermons throughout the thirteen colonies, sometimes to as many as thirty thousand people at once. Wherever he went, Whitfield shared the good news that Jesus Christ had come for sinners and that all a sinner needed to do was repent, accept the atoning death of Jesus for his sins, and trust Jesus with his life.[4]

Through his preaching, and that of Jonathan Edwards, William Tennent, and others, revival came to every American colony, and almost every American home. It has been estimated that of a colonial population of one million in 1740, several thousand to half a million Americans were converted.[5]

While some attributed the revival to the need exposed by a diphtheria epidemic, to tensions of generations over division of diminishing amounts of land, and to the desire for personal peace and an escape from guilt, most regarded it as a "...special outpouring of the Holy Spirit."[6]

Since, historically, the realization of need precedes the sovereign grace of God, all these things probably contributed to the repentance that swept the colonies. Certainly there was again in the land the teaching of Calvin.

This great revival led inevitably to the founding of many Christian Colleges--among them the College of New Jersey (now Princeton), Rhode Island College (now Brown University), Queens College (now Rutgers), and Dartmouth.[7]

"At the time of the Declaration of Independence the quality of education had enabled the colonies to achieve a degree of literacy from 70% to virtually 100%..." wrote Moses Coit Tyler, historian of American literature. "This was not education restricted to the few. Modern scholarship reports the prevalence of schooling and its accessibility to all segments of the population. The colonists' familiarity with history, extensive legal learning...lucid exposition of Constitutional principles, show, indeed, that somehow out into the American wilderness had been carried the very accent of cosmolitan thought and speech. When the American State papers arrived in Europe...they were found to contain nearly every quality indicative of personal and national greatness."[8]

Converted, united in the Christian faith, and studying *The Bible* again--as had the first English settlers--the colonists had a consensus of opinion commonly shared by all and were spiritually and intellectually prepared for the test that was soon to come from the King and Parliament of England.

"The Great Awakening," which has been called our national conversion, resulted in the thirteen colonies becoming the first nation ever to be founded as a Christian nation in the history of mankind. Thanks to the teaching of John Calvin, "One Nation Under God" became true for America not only spiritually, but politically.

For the first time, the colonists began to see all were equal at the foot of the cross and, in the sight of God who is no respecter of persons, a farmer was as good as King George. They came to see that the brotherhood of man came from being born again into the family of God and becoming His children through that new birth--that Liberty, Equality, and Fraternity are gifts from God. (Without God, as the French Revolution was later to show, Liberty, Equality, and Fraternity could only result in carnage and evil.) Moreover, the Americans were willing to defend these gifts with their lives, if necessary.

"America is a nation with the soul of a church," wrote Sidney Mead. The ministers, who had a tremendous influence on the people, were almost all behind the resistance of the colonies and began to say, "The cause of America is the cause of Christ."[9]

The other event that prepared the colonists for the Revolution was the French and Indian War which ended in 1770. It taught them how to fight and that they could win.

At the same time, it was this war that opened the door to the British illegal abuse of maintaining a standing army in the colonies and taxing the colonies to support it; the forbidding of the settling of lands west of the Appalachian Mountains; the Writs of Assistance (search warrants to prevent importation of raw materials in order to prevent development of manufacturing industries in the colonies); the Quartering Act of 1765 which required the colonials to provide food, housing, and transportation for British troops stationed in the colonies; and the Stamp Act, requiring them to buy stamps and affix to newspapers, legal documents, and other papers.

The fact was the Americans were being taxed for Britain's own revenue and, which was worse, being denied the right of all Englishmen to representation in the government which was taxing them as well as equality of opportunity.

Confronted with a king who demanded total submission, once again the colonists heard freedom preached throughout the land. A favorite text of the ministers was, "For freedom, Christ has set us free: stand fast, therefore, and do not submit again to a yoke of slavery."[10]

Patrick Henry denounced the acts of King George III as contrary to the English *Magna Charta* and *The Bill of Rights,* and usurping the citizenship of the American colonists. The Stamp Act Congress was convened in October, 1765, consisting of delegates from nine of the thirteen colonies. They approved a Declaration of Rights and sent petitions to the king and British Parliament protesting the Stamp Act. It was repealed in 1766, but at the same time Parliament maintained it had the right to enforce any laws it pleased concerning the colonies. To prove it, they promptly imposed the Townsend Act which taxed imports from the colonies.

The Virginia legislature passed resolutions against this act and was promptly dissolved by the royal governor. Moving to a nearby town, they adopted a non-importation, non-exportation agreement. This boycott spread throughout the colonies, and in 1770 the British Parliament repealed all the Townsend taxes except the tax on tea.

That year "The Boston Massacre" occurred. Angered by the stationing of British troops in Boston, a mob attacked a squad of British soldiers who responded by firing on the crowd, killing three and wounding eight--two of whom later died of their wounds. John Adams took the very unpopular case for the British soldiers, risking his political career by so doing. At the same time, he proved he believed in law and not in mob rule It didn't hurt his popularity, for shortly after he was elected to the Massachusetts General Court (legislature)--showing most of the people must have agreed with his stand against mob rule also.[11]

Shortly after the Stamp Act was repealed, Jonathan Mayhew of Boston predicted in a sermon that one day Americans might be the salvation of the mother country that was seeking to oppress them--a prophecy those of us who lived during the Second World War saw fulfilled. He said:

"God gave the Israelites a king in His anger, because they had not sense and virtue enough to like a free commonwealth, and to have Himself for their king...the Son of God came down from heaven to make us 'free indeed,' and that 'where the Spirit of the Lord is, there is liberty,' who knows, our liberties being thus established, but that on some future occasion, when the kingdoms of earth are moved; and roughly dashed one against another...we, or our posterity, may even have the great felicity and honor to 'save much people alive,' and keep Britian herself from ruin!"[12]

"The Father of the American Revolution," Samuel Adams, who had the upbringing and deep religious convictions of a Puritan, wrote the first document that questioned the right of the British Parliament to tax the colonies without their consent. He also suggested the need for a meeting of representatives of all the colonies to decide on a united course of action--a suggestion that led to the Stamp Act Congress. He became a leading spirit in the Sons of Liberty and was a ring-leader in the Boston Teaparty.

When London imposed a tax on tea imported into the colonies and sent three shiploads to Boston, patriots had to face the fact that "Taxation without representation is tyranny," and that tyranny leads inevitably to the loss of all freedoms. They knew if Americans bought the tea and paid the tax, they would be accepting the principle that Britain could tax them without representation.

Summoned by church bells on December 16, 1773, they spoke of how "...tea will mingle with salt water," and Boston Harbor become "...a teapot tonight." Disguised as Mohawks, and even unknown to each other behind the blackened faces, the "Sons of Liberty" boarded the *Dartmouth,* the *Eleanor*, and the *Beaver* while a large crowd watched from the wharf. The people were so silent they could hear the sound of hatchets breaking open the caskets of tea and the splash as they were dumped into the harbor. The Boston Tea Party was over in three hours, but the memory of it never left the colonists...or the citizens of the United States.[13]

The following day, John Adams wrote in his diary, "There is a Dignity, a Majesty, a Sublimity in this last effort of the Patriots that I greatly admire. This Destruction of the Tea is so bold, so daring, so firm, intrepid, and inflexible, and it must have so important consequences and so lasting that I cannot but consider it as an Epoch in History."[14]

The colonists had struggled for many years over the spiritual implications of a break with England. Their ministers had preached the Word of God on this question, reminding them that their forefathers had come to this land because they were not free to worship God and live according to His Word in Europe. Now the warning that their freedoms were again threatened came from the pulpits of America.

The British responded to the Tea Party by imposing Intolerable Acts and closing Boston Harbor. The most prosperous port in America now faced financial ruin and sympathy for Boston rapidly spread throughout the colonies. Summoned by Committees of Correspondence, the First Continental Congress convened in Philadelphia on September 5, 1774, with delegates from all the colonies except Georgia and Canada. They sent resolutions to the King and Parliament asking that their rights as British citizens be respected and, at the same time, they instituted a means of enforcing a boycott.

The following year they met again at Old St. John's Church in Richmond, because the royal governor forbade the meeting of the Virginia Legislature. It was in their meeting at this church on March 23, 1775 that Patrick Henry spoke his ringing words:

"...There is no longer room for hope. If we wish to be free, we must fight! An appeal to arms and to the God of Hosts is all that is left us!...Three million people, armed in the holy cause of liberty and in such a country as that which we possess, are invincible by any force which our enemy can send against us. Besides, we shall not fight our battles alone. There is a just God who presides over the destinies of nations, and who will raise up friends for us. The battle, sir, is not to the strong alone; it is to the vigilant, the active, the brave...There is no retreat but in submission and slavery! Our chains are forged. Their clanking may be heard on the plains of Boston! The war is inevitable--let it come!...

"Gentlemen may cry, peace, peace--but there is no peace. The war is actually begun! The next gale that sweeps from the north will bring to our ears the clashing of resounding arms! Our brethren are already in the field! Why stand we here idle?...Is life so dear, or peace so sweet, as to be purchased at the price of chains and slavery? Forbid it, Almighty God! I know not what course others may take; but as for me, give me liberty, or give me death!"[15]

Writing The Declaration of Independence
J.T.L. Ferris, Archives of 76, Bay Village, Ohio

CHAPTER FOUR

Who Were These Revolutionaries?

Who were these revolutionaries who gave us our Declaration of Independence? John Adams, "The Atlas of the Revolution," described them as "...such an assembly as never before came together on a sudden, in any part of the world; here were fortunes, ability, learning, eloquence, acuteness equal to any I ever met with in my life. Here is a diversity of religions, impossible to unite on one line of conduct."[1]

But all acknowledged God and took the Bible to be the measure of what is right and most of them, or their ancestors, had come to this country to escape the religious persecution they had endured in Europe for practicing and sharing this Biblical faith. It was on this faith in God's Word as the only measure of truth that they had found a consensus of opinion that enabled them to agree on the essentials and to found a Christian nation they described on their Great Seal, coins, and paper money as *E Pluribus Unum--One From Many*. Eventually it became known as the greatest nation on earth--a nation which was to draw liberty-loving people from all over the world. Jesus Christ promised, "If I be lifted up, I will draw all men unto me," and the fact is most of them were "revolutionaries for Christ" who wanted freedom to worship Him.

They were elected representatives of the thirteen colonies and dedicated patriots. They were men who pledged their lives, their fortunes, and their sacred honor in signing The Declaration of Independence. Not one lost his life in battle, or his honor, though many gave their fortunes.

They were leaders: two became Presidents of the United States; two became Vice-Presidents; three became Supreme Court Justices; five became State Supreme Court Justices; one became Secretary of State; one became United States Treasurer; six became

United States Senators; three became Members of the House of Representatives; and ten became Governors of their states. Many of their descendants became great leaders in various fields of endeavor.

They were educated: eight at Harvard, four at Yale, four at William & Mary, three at Philadelphia (University of Pennsylvania), two at Princeton (College of New Jersey)--all colleges whose charters stated they were established for the advancement of the Christian faith; seven were educated in France or England, and two at the University of Edinburgh. One was President of the College of New Jersey, one became Chancellor of the University of Virginia.

They were fighters: two were Commanders-in-Chief of their State Militia; one was Brigadier-General of the Continental Army; one was the top executive officer of the American Navy. Some died before the war ended; some were taken prisoners of war; but none were killed in battle.[2]

They were deeply religious men: John Hancock, President of the Continental Congress, who signed with such a large flourish that his name became synonymous with the word "signature," was born in a parsonage, the son and grandson of Puritan ministers. He put up one-quarter million dollars to help finance the war, and said, "Burn Boston and make John Hancock a pauper if the public good requires." He described the British troops as "...men whom sceptered robbers now employ to frustrate the design of God and render vain the bounties which His gracious hand passes indiscriminately upon his creatures."[3]

He warned, "We must all hang together," to which Benjamin Franklin replied, "Yes, we must indeed all hang together, or most assuredly we shall all hang separately."[4]

The oldest man to sign the Declaration of Independence and the oldest to sign the Constitution, Benjamin Franklin was to play an important part in saving the Constitutional Convention from failure. In the spring of 1787, this Convention was deadlocked, a feeling of discouragement prevailed, and men from various states were planning to leave. Then Franklin stood to his feet and, addressing George Washington who was presiding, said, "Sir, we have not hitherto once thought of humbly appealing to the father of lights to illuminate our understanding. In the beginning of the contest with Great Britain, when we were sensible to danger, we had daily prayers in this room for Divine protection. Our prayers, Sir, were heard and they were graciously answered...Do we imagine that we no longer need His assistance? I have lived, Sir, a long time and the longer I live, the more convincing proofs I see of this truth--that God governs in the affairs of man. And if a sparrow cannot fall to the ground without His notice, (quoting Jesus, Matthew 10:29) is it probable an empire can rise without His aid? We have been assured, sir, in the sacred writings, that except the Lord build the house, they labor in vain that build it...(Psalm 127:1) I firmly believe this..."[5]

They went on to give us a constitution that has outlasted most governments of the world and stood the test of time. It has drawn people from every part of the earth "...yearning to be free."

Franklin's father had come to America in 1683 seeking religious freedom. He had carried Benjamin across the street to the Old South Church to be baptized the day he was born.[6]

While he was under his father's care, he had to attend public worship and family prayers. The grandson of an indentured servant who his grandfather had bought for twenty pounds and afterwards married, Benjamin was also indentured to his older brother as a printer apprentice when he was twelve, but after five years of not getting along with him, ran away to Philadelphia.[7]

Shortly before Benjamin Franklin's death, he shared his faith with a friend: "Death is as necessary to the constitution as sleep. We shall rise refreshed in the morning. The course of nature must soon put a period to my present mode of existence. This I shall submit to with the less regret, as having seen, during a long life, a good deal of this world, I feel a growing curiosity to become acquainted with some other; and can cheerfully, with filial confidence, resign my spirit to the conduct of that great and good Parent of mankind, who created it, and who has so graciously protected and preserved me from my birth to the present hour."[8]

About six weeks before his death, he wrote Ezra Stiles, President of Yale, "You desire to know something of my religion...Here is my creed. I believe in one God, creator of the universe. That

He governs it by His providence. That He ought to be worshiped. That the most acceptable service we render Him is doing good to His other children. That the soul of man is immortal, and will be treated with justice in another life respecting its conduct in this. These I take to be the fundamental principles of all sound religion, and I regard them as you do in whatever sect I meet with them.

"As to Jesus of Nazareth, my opinion of whom you particularly desire, I think the system of morals and his religion, as he left them to us, the best the world ever saw or is likely to see; but I apprehend it has received various corrupt changes, and I have, with most of the present Dissenters in England, some doubts as to his divinity; though it is a question I do not dogmatize upon, *having never studied it* (italics mine) and think it needless to busy myself with it now, when I expect soon an opportunity of knowing the truth with less trouble. I see no harm, however, in its being believed, if that belief has the good consequence, as probably it has, of making his doctrines more respected and better observed...

"I shall only add, respecting myself, that, having experienced the goodness of that Being in conducting me prosperously through a long life, I have no doubt of its continuance in the next, without the smallest conceit of meriting it...All sects here, and we have a great variety, have experienced my good will in assisting them with subscriptions for building their new places of worship; and, as I never opposed any of their doctrines, I hope to go out of the world in peace with them all."

His wish to go out of this world in peace with all the churches was granted. First in the cortege from Franklin's house to Christ Church in Philadelphia where he was buried, went all the clergy of the city because Franklin had aided all the churches![9]

(How he fared in the next only God knows, but it does seem a shame this man who had such an inquiring mind and started the first library in America never took the time to study what *The Bible* says about the divinity of Jesus and how to get to heaven.)

The only clergyman to sign the Declaration was John Witherspoon, direct descendant of John Knox, the founder of Protestantism in Scotland. The son of a Presbyterian clergyman, he had been a leading Presbyterian minister in Scotland where he had taken part in an unsuccessful revolution in the 1740's. He had come to America in 1768 as President of the College of New Jersey. There he taught James Madison who later became known as the "Father of the Constitution."

Witherspoon arrived in Philadelphia as a delegate to the Continental Congress in June, 1776, just in time to hear the debate over independence between John Adams and John Dickinson. Said to have more presence than anyone except George Washington, he responded to the remark that the colonies were "...not yet ripe for a declaration of independence...," by declaring, "In my judgment, sir, we are not only ripe, but rotting."

A leader of the Presbyterian Church, Witherspoon helped organize and presided over the opening session of the first General Assembly of that church in 1789. His essays and his sermons on theological subjects were widely read, and he gave important guidance for the Constitution of the United States and the Constitution of the American Presbyterian Church, which were both written the same year and by some of the same people.[10]

There was Samuel Adams, who said, "Our cause is righteous,and we shall never be abandoned by Heaven while we show ourselves worthy of its aid and protection."

A leading spirit in the Sons of Liberty, he also started the committees of correspondence which provided the communications network essential for united action in the revolutionary cause.

As a young man he had wanted to become a Christian minister, but instead he became "The Father of the American Revolution."

Of his cousin, John Adams wrote, "Without the character of Samuel Adams, the true history of the American Revolution can never be written. For 50 years, his pen, his tongue, his activity were consistently exerted for his country without fee or reward."[11]

John Adams was a descendant of John Alden of the Pilgrim band who landed at Plymouth that harsh winter of 1620, and of a Puritan who left England in 1640 seeking religious freedom.

He had his differences with Jefferson, just as his forefathers had their differences with the Church of England. After Washington had served his two terms, both ran for the presidency. In the midst of a heated campaign, marked by much name-calling and mud-slinging, Jefferson wrote of John Adams, "The measure of the general government are a fair subject for difference of opinion, but do not found your opinions on the notion that there is the smallest speck of dishonesty, moral or political, in the character of John Adams, for I know him well, and I repeat that a man more perfectly honest never issued from the hands of his creator."[12]

The only Roman Catholic to sign the declaration was Charles Carroll of Maryland. Also one of the three wealthiest men in America, George Washington of Virginia and Henry Middleton of South Carolina being the other two, he gladly risked his life and his fortune for the cause of liberty and religious freedom. Tracing his ancestry to the ancient kings of Ireland, he lived in an aristocratic manner that befitted kings. His ancestor, the first Charles Carroll, came to Maryland in 1688 and received large land grants that became the basis of the family fortune.

Because Catholics in Maryland were denied all political, religious, and educational freedom, his father took him to France to receive a Catholic education. (His cousin, John J. Carroll, later became the first Roman Catholic Bishop in America.)

In recognition for his zeal for independence, the state convention of Maryland appointed him as a representative to the Continental Congress on July 4, 1776, not knowing, because of the poor communication of the day, that Congress had already approved independence.

When the engrossed copy of The Declaration of Independence was laid before the Congress on August 2, Hancock asked Carroll if he cared to sign since he was not present at its adoption.

"Most willingly," he replied. As he signed, one of the other delegates is reported to have said, "There goes a few millions!" referring to the fortune Carroll risked losing by placing himself on record as a traitor in the eyes of the British. He was the last surviving signer, dying at the age of 95 on November 14, 1832.[13]

Although threatened that "…their necks might be inconveniently lengthened," none of them were killed during the Revolution, and their average lifespan was 65 years.

There was no "generation gap." The signers varied in age from 26 to 81, their average age being 42. They were family men--all but two were married, and they averaged six children per father.[14]

All but eight were native-born--sixteen in the northeastern colonies, fourteen in the middle Atlantic, and eighteen in the southern colonies. Two were from England, one from Wales, two from Scotland, and three from Ireland.[15]

From so many backgrounds, these valiant men brought forth the United States of America--"One nation, under God indivisible, with liberty and justice for all."

We have fallen into repeating our Pledge of Allegiance as if there were a comma after God, missing the whole point these courageous signers of the Declaration of Independence understood so well--that only as we are submitted to God and His Word will we be indivisible. Our founding fathers understood this and put it in our motto, "In God We Trust" and in the Declaration of Independence. They knew Him to be the source of our "...inalienable (that cannot be taken away from us) rights..." rights that were God-given, and God-protected, for which "...with a firm reliance on the providence of God..." they were willing to risk "their lives, their fortunes and their sacred honor."[16]

Samuel Adams

John Adams

Benjamin Franklin

Thomas Jefferson

CHAPTER FIVE

Two Proclamations--
What Price Liberty?

After the Battles of Lexington and Concord and the capture of Fort Ticonderoga, two proclamations were made on June 12, 1775. One, by the Second Continental Congress meeting in Philadelphia, called for a day of fasting and prayer. It read:

"As the Great Governor of the World, by his supreme and universal Providence, not only conducts the course of nature with unerring wisdom and rectitude, but frequently influences the minds of men to serve the wise and gracious purposes of His indispensable duty, devoutly to acknowledge His superintending Providence, especially in times of impending danger, and public calamity, to reverence and adore his immutable Justice, as well as to implore his merciful Interposition for our deliverance.

"This Congress, therefore, considering the present critical, alarming and calamitous state of these Colonies, do earnestly recommend, that Thursday, the Twentieth day of July next, be observed by the Inhabitants of all the English Colonies on this Continent, as a day of public HUMILIATION, FASTING AND PRAYER, that we may with united hearts and voices, unfeignedly confess and deplore our many sins and offer up our joint supplications to the All-wise, Omnipotent and merciful Disposer of all Events, humbly beseeching Him to forgive our iniquities, to remove our present calamities, to avert the desolating judgments with which we are threatened, and to bless our rightful Sovereign King George the IIId. and inspire him with wisdom to discern and pursue the true interest of all his subjects--that a speedy end may be put to the civil discord between Great Britain and the American Colonies, without further effusion of blood--and that the British nation may be influenced in regard to the *things that* belong to her peace, before they are hid from her eyes--that these Colonies may be ever under the care and protection of a kind Providence, and be prospered in all their interests--that the divine Blessing may descend and rest upon all our civil Rulers, and upon the Representatives of the people in their several Assemblies and Conventions, that they may be directed to wise and effectual measures for preserving the Union and securing the just Rights and Privileges of the Colonies--that virtue and true religion may revive and flourish throughout our land--and that America may soon behold a gracious interposition of Heaven for the redress of her many grievances, the restoration of her invaded Rights, a reconciliation with the the parent State, on terms constitutional and honorable to both--and that her civil and religious Privileges may be secured to the latest posterity. And it is recommended to Christians of all denominations to assemble for public worship, and to abstain from servile Labour and Recreations on said day. By order of the Congress, John Hancock, President."[1]

The other proclamation was by British General Gage who was stationed in Boston. It called for martial law in the province of Massachusetts and singled out Samuel Adams and John Hancock for capture and trial in England--a fate from which, fortunately, they narrowly escaped.[2]

The colonists had met with the news of the battles of Lexington and Concord ringing in their ears. Nothing could have united them more quickly than the response of the British in closing the Boston port.

William Prescott, who later led the patriot forces at the Battle of Bunker Hill, wrote the Boston patriots, "We heartily sympathize with you, and are always ready to do all in our power for your support, comfort and relief, knowing that Providence has placed you where you must stand the first shock. We consider that we are all embarked in this and must sink or swim together...Our forefathers passed the vast Atlantic, spent their blood and treasure, that they might enjoy their liberties, both civil and religious, and transmit them to their posterity...How if we should give them up, can our children rise up and call us blessed?...Let us all be of one heart, and stand fast in the liberty wherewith Christ has made us free. And may He, of His infinite mercy, grant us deliverance out of all our troubles."[3]

The Governor of Massachusetts, John Hancock, called for prayer and repentance at their State Provincial Congress, saying, "We think it is incumbent upon this people to humble themselves before God on account of their sins,...and implore the Divine Blessing upon us, that by the assistance of His grace, we may be enabled to reform whatever is amiss among us..." Addressing the inhabitants of Massachusetts Bay, he said, "Resistance to tyranny becomes the Christian and social duty of each individual... Continue steadfast and, with a proper sense of your dependence on God, nobly defend those rights which heaven gave, and no man ought to take away."[4]

Three weeks after the taking of Fort Ticonderoga, the Reverend Samuel Langdon, President of Harvard College, spoke at the Provincial Congress of Massachusetts. Realizing his sermon would be printed and read throughout the colonies, he said, "We have rebelled against God. We have lost the true spirit of Christianity, though we retain the outward profession and form of it. We have neglected and set light by the glorious Gospel of our Lord Jesus Christ and His holy commands and institutions. The worship of many is but mere compliment to the Deity, while their hearts are far from Him. By many the Gospel is corrupted into a superficial system of moral philosophy, little better than ancient Platonism." (He was referring to Deism, which was undermining the Trinitarian understanding of Christianity and leading to a watered-down belief in God as an impersonal Higher Being and the denial of the deity of Christ and the necessity of His death on the cross to pay the penalty for our sins.)

Referring to the war, President Langdon asked, "Wherefore is all this evil upon us? Is it not because we have forsaken the Lord? ...let us repent and implore the divine mercy. Let us amend our ways and our doings, reform everything that has been provoking the Most High, and thus endeavor to obtain the gracious interpositions of providence for our deliverance...

"If God be for us, who can be against us?...May our land be purged from all its sins! Then the Lord will be our refuge and our strength, a very present help in trouble, and we will have no reason to be afraid, though thousands of enemies set themselves against us round about..."[5]

Almost all of the governors, who had been appointed by King George III. remained loyal to the crown. However, Governor Trumbull of Connecticut said, "It is hard to break connections with our mother country, but when she strives to enslave us, the strictest union must be dissolved....The Lord reigneth." Another colonial governor wrote the Board of Trade in England, "If you ask any American, who is his master? He will tell you he has none, nor any governor, but Jesus Christ." Word was passed throughout the colonies by Committees of Correspondence, and soon the cry, "No king but King Jesus!" was heard throughout the land.[6]

General Gage had been instructed to put down the rebellion at once, and immediately sent 700 redcoats to confiscate the military supplies the patriots had stored at Concord. Paul Revere and William Davis rode all night spreading the news, "The British are coming!" American Minutemen were waiting for them with the order from their Captain Parker, "Stand your ground. Don't fire unless fired upon, but if they mean to have a war, let it begin here."

On that historic day, April 19, 1775, "...the shot heard 'round the world..." was fired by a trigger-happy British soldier. The War of Independence had begun.

The Battle of Lexington and Concord ended with an ignominious rout of the British and a clear victory for the colonists. The confidence of the Americans soared as they realized they had stood up to the best British troops and had given them a beating.

Almost immediately Colonel Matthew Arnold and Colonel Ethan Allen, with 83 men, crossed Lake Champlain and to their amazement found the gate to Ft. Ticonderoga open. The British sentry fired at one of them pointblank, but his gun failed to go off.

They woke the fort's commander and ordered, "Deliver this fort instantly!"

"By what authority?" he asked.

"In the name of the great Jehovah and the Continental Congress," shouted Allen, raising his sword over the captain's head, whereupon he promptly surrendered.[7]

Realizing the importance of Samuel Adams, but totally under-estimating his character, Governor Gage sent a military aide to try to bribe him to stop his patriotic efforts. Adams listened carefully and sent his reply, "I trust I have long since made my peace with the King of Kings. No personal consideration shall induce me to abandon the righteous cause of my country. Tell Governor Gage it is the advice of Samuel Adams to him no longer to insult the feelings of an exasperated people."

In 1772,he had written, "Just and true liberty, equal impartial liberty, in matters spiritual and temporary, is a thing that all men are clearly entitled to by the eternal and immutable laws of God and nature, as well as by the law of nations and all well-grounded municipal laws, which must have their foundation in the former."[8]

After Gage's attempt to bribe him, he wrote a friend in Boston, "I am perfectly satisfied of the necessity of a public and explicit declaration of independence. I cannot conceive what good reason can be assigned against it..."

When the Second Continental Congress convened in Philadelphia, the news of Lexington and Concord was foremost in their thoughts and conversation. They appointed George Washington Commander-in-Chief of the Continental Army and he went immediately to Boston's outskirts where the colonists had just won an amazing victory at the Battle of Bunker Hill...until they ran out of ammunition and had to retreat. In the spring of 1776, the Virginia assembly authorized its delegates in Philadelphia to urge Congress to declare the colonies free of Great Britain. Richard Henry Lee of Virginia wrote a brief paper and presented it on June 7. He concluded the introduction of his bill by saying:

"Why, then, sir, why do we longer delay? Why still deliberate? Let this happy day give birth to an American republic. Let her arise, not to devastate and to conquer, but to re-establish the reign of peace and of law. The eyes of Europe are fixed upon us: she demands of us a living example of freedom, that may exhibit a contrast, in the felicity of the citizen, to the ever-increasing tyranny which desolates her polluted shores. She invites us to prepare an asylum where the unhappy may find solace, and the persecuted repose. She entreats us to cultivate a propitious soil, where that

79

generous plant which first sprung and grew in England, but is now withered by the poisonous blasts of Scottish tyranny, may revive and flourish, sheltering under its salubrious and interminable shade all the unfortunate of the race..."[9]

His bill was seconded by John Adams and opposed by John J. Dickinson of Pennsylvania and Robert Livingston, Jr., of New York, who still clung to the hope of reconciliation with Great Britain.

On June 10, Congress decided to postpone further consideration of Lee's resolution until July 1, but to appoint a committee to write a declaration of independence. That same day Lee was called home because of the serious illness of his wife, and was absent when his resolution was adopted.[10]

In his first speech to the Virginia House of Burgesses at the age of twenty-five, he had supported the abolition of slavery, saying, "...Christianity, by introducing into Europe the truest principles of humanity, universal benevolence, and brotherly love, had happily abolished civil slavery. Let us, who profess the same religion, practice its precepts, and by agreeing to this duty, convince the world that we know and practice our true interests, and that we pay a proper regard to the dictates of justice and humanity."[11]

Had the Colonists heeded his words, we might have been spared the agony of the Civil War. (They probably reasoned they had trouble enough rousing support for their cause, but history has shown again and again that this is a moral universe and, sooner or later, our moral compromises catch up with us.)

Lee was also present at the meeting of the Virginia Assembly in Old Saint John's Church in Richmond in March of 1775 when Patrick Henry thrilled his listeners with his cry, "Give me liberty, or give me death!" and supported him by saying, "Admitting the probable calculations to be against us, we are assured in holy writ, that the race is not to the swift, nor the battle to the strong; and if the language of genius may be added to that of inspiration, I will say with our immortal bard,

"Thrice is he armed, who hath his quarrel just

And he but naked, tho' locked in steel,

Whose conscience with injustice is oppressed."[12]

Thus Richard Henry Lee of Virginia laid our War of Independence on the solid rock of faith in the righteousness of our cause.

As chairman of the committee that prepared Washington's commission and instructions as Commander-in-Chief of the Continental Army, Lee wrote the following address to the people of Great Britain:

"The great bulwarks of our (English) Constitution we have desired to maintain by every temperate, by every peaceable means; but your ministers, equal foes to British and American freedom, have added to their former oppressions an attempt to reduce us by the sword to a base and abject submission. On the sword, therefore, we are compelled to rely for protection. Should victory declare in your favor, yet men trained to arms from their infancy and animated by the love of liberty, will afford neither a cheap nor easy conquest. Of this at least we are assured, that our struggle will be glorious, our success certain; since even in death we shall find that freedom which in life you forbid us to enjoy."[13]

Reading the Declaration of Independence from East Balcony,
State House, Boston, 1776

CHAPTER SIX

"...Proclaim Liberty Throughout the Land ..."

On July 1, 1776, John Adams responded to those who spoke eloquently and at length against independence:

"Before God, I believe the hour has come. My judgment approves this measure, and my whole heart is in it. All that I have, and all that I am, and all that I hope in this life, I am now ready here to stake upon it. And I leave off as I began, that live or die, survive or perish, I am for the Declaration. It is my living sentiment, and by the blessing of God it shall be my dying sentiment, Independence now, and Independence forever!" Fifty years later, a few days before his death, he was asked what toast should be given at the 50th anniversary of the Declaration of Independence. His response was, "Independence forever!"[1]

Both he and Thomas Jefferson, the two men most responsible for The Declaration of Independence, died on the 50th anniversary of that historic document, a coincidence that seemed most significant to the new nation.[2]

From the beginning, the representatives of the Continental Congress saw themselves as a legitimate government seeking to separate itself from an illegitimate government which was usurping their rights as British citizens.

They had petitioned the king for redress of grievances, of which they had a long list. Having come to the colonies to escape oppressive restrictions on their religious freedom, they protested that now King George III was violating the rights guaranteed to them by the original charters Britain had granted them when they left England. Their first act at the First Continental Congress had been to pass the following resolution: "Resolved, That the Rev.

Mr. Duche be desired to open Congress to-morrow morning with prayer, at Carpenter's Hall, at nine o'clock."

On the day after the first official session of the First Continental Congress, September 7, 1774, John Adams wrote his wife, Abigail, "You must remember this was the morning after we heard the horrible rumor of the cannonade of Boston. I never saw a greater effect upon an audience. It seemed as if heaven had ordained that psalm to be read on that morning. After this Mr. Duche unexpectedly to everybody struck out into an extemporary prayer which filled the bosom of every man present...It had an excellent effect upon everybody here."

This is the prayer he prayed, and it was gloriously answered in the years that followed:

"O Lord our Heavenly Father, high and mighty King of Kings and Lord of Lords who dost from Thy throne behold all the dwellers on earth, and reignest with power supreme and uncontrolled over all kingdoms, empires and governments; look down in mercy we beseech Thee, on these American States, who have fled to Thee from the rod of the oppressor, and thrown themselves on Thy gracious protection, desiring to be henceforth dependent only on Thee; to Thee they have appealed for the righteousness of their cause; to Thee do they now look up for that countenance and support which Thou alone canst give; take them therefore, Heavenly Father, under Thy nurturing care; give them wisdom in council, and valor in the field; defeat the malicious designs of our cruel adversaries, convince them of the unrighteousness of their cause; and if they still persist in their sanguinary purposes, O let the voice of Thine own unerring justice sounding in their hearts constrain them to drop the weapons of war from their unnerved hands in the day of battle. Be Thou present, O God of wisdom, and direct the councils of this honorable assembly; enable them to settle things on the best and surest foundation, that the scene of blood may be speedily closed, that order, harmony, and peace, may be effectually restored; and truth and justice, religion and piety, prevail and flourish amongst Thy people. Preserve the health of their bodies and the vigor of their minds; shower down on them and the millions they here represent, such temporal blessings as Thou seest expedient for them in this world and crown them with everlasting glory in the world to come. All this we ask in the name and through the merits of Jesus Christ, Thy Son, our Saviour. Amen."[3]

Two years later, after many violations of their rights as British citizens, the Second Continental Congress appointed a committee to explain their position to America, to Britain, and to the world, and to draft a declaration of independence. The committee, consisting of Thomas Jefferson, John Adams, Benjamin Franklin, Robert Sherman, and Robert R. Livingston, voted for young Jefferson to do the writing because of his talent with words. His own story was published by Julian P. Boyd, the editor of his Papers:

"The committee for drawing the Declaration of Independence desired me to do it. It was accordingly done and being approved by them, I reported it to the house on Friday, the 28th of June, when it was read and ordered to lie on the table."

Adams explained his appointment by the committee:

"I gave him my vote and did all in my power to procure the vote of others. I think he had one more vote than any other, and that placed him at the head of the committee. I had the next highest number, and that placed me second." (In other words, had Adams voted for himself, he would have been the writer of the Declaration instead of Jefferson.)[4]

On July 1, Adams, who was called "The Atlas of American Independence," presented to the Continental Congress the reasons why independence should be declared. Jefferson later described Adam's presentation as, "...not graceful or eloquent, nor remarkably fluent, but he gave out occasionally a power of thought and expression that moved us from our seats."[5]

Jefferson sat silently as the delegates acted as a board of editors. Thirty-nine changes were made in the short document by the Congressional delegates. They deleted more words than they added, so the document ended more concise than when it was submitted by Jefferson. His draft included only a reference to "nature's God" but, when it was threshed out in committee, Adams, Franklin, Livingston, and Sherman added the important words, "they are endowed by their Creator with certain inalienable rights," knowing the only rights that are inalienable are those given by God. When the Declaration was debated on the floor of the Congress, the phrases, "...appealing to the Supreme Judge of the world, for the rectitude of our intentions..." and "...with a firm reliance on the protection of divine Providence," were added, bringing the Declaration into harmony with the Christian consensus of the majority of the members of the Continental Congress and the colonists who knew the Bible named Jesus as the Supreme Judge of the world."[6]

Nine of the Colonies voted for, Pennsylvania and South Carolina voted no, and New York abstained, while Delaware was split. But Caesar Rodney, who had been away serving as brigadier general in command of Delaware's militia, rode 89 miles through a terrible torrent and arrived at 1:00 P.M. just as the final vote was being taken. Half carried into the room, he was barely able to speak the words he had come to say, "I vote for Independence."

Rodney had cancer on his face and had been planning to go to England to see the only doctor in the world known to have any treatment for it. In casting this vote, he was giving up his only chance to be cured, and he died at the age of fifty, literally giving his life for the cause.[7]

After the signing, some were silent; some wept openly; some bowed their heads and closed their eyes to pray. John Hancock said, "Gentlemen, the price on my head has just been doubled!" But the Father of the American Revolution, Samuel Adams, rose and said, "We have this day restored the Sovereign, to Whom alone men ought to be obedient. He reigns in heaven and...from the rising to the setting sun, may his Kingdom come."

Americans everywhere were jubilant over the news. Church bells rang, people cheered, waved, and fired precious ammunition.

"The people, I am told, recognize the resolution as though it were a decree promulgated from heaven," wrote John Adams. He was so excited he wrote his wife, Abigail, twice on July 2. In the first letter, he anticipated the furnace of affliction, but said, it "...produces refinements in states, as well as individuals." In the second he predicted that independence day "...will be the most memorable...in the history of America. I am apt to believe that it will be celebrated by succeeding generations, as the great anniversary festival. It ought to be commemorated as the Day of Deliverance, by solemn acts of devotion to God Almighty. It ought to be solemnized with pomp and parade, with shows, games, sports, guns, bells, bonfires and illuminations, from one end of this continent to the other, from this time forward forevermore.

"You will think me transported with enthusiasm, but I am not. I am well aware of the toil and blood and treasure that it will cost to maintain this Declaration, and support and defend these States. Yet through all the gloom I can see the rays of light and glory. I can see that the end is worth more than all the means; and that posterity will triumph, although you and I may rue, which I hope we shall not."[8]

On the day the Declaration was passed, General Howe landed on Staten Island with the first of what would eventually be fifty-five thousand troops. Although the American soldiers continued to report miraculous and supernatural aid, all seemed lost for the Colonial Army by the following winter.

George Washington, who credited Thomas Paine's pamphlet, *Common Sense,* with bringing about the signing of the Declaration of Independence, asked him to write *The American Crisis,* and he wrote:,

"These are the times that try men's souls: The summer soldier and the sunshine patriot will, in this crises, shrink from the service of their country; but he that stands it now, deserves the love and thanks of man and woman. Tyranny, like hell, is not easily conquered; yet we have this consolation with us, that the harder the conflict, the more glorious the triumph. What we obtain too cheap, we esteem too lightly; it is dearness only that gives everything its value. Heaven knows how to put a proper price upon its goods; and it would be strange indeed if so celestial an article as FREEDOM should not be highly rated. Britain, with an army to enforce her tyranny, has declared that she has a right *(not only to* TAX) but "to BIND us in CASES WHATSOEVER," and if being *bound in that manner, is not slavery, then there is not such a thing as slavery upon earth. Even the expression is impious, for so unlimited a power can belong only to God...*

"I have as little superstition in me as any man living, but my secret opinion has ever been, and still is, that God Almighty will not give up a people to military destruction, or leave them unsupportedly to perish, who have so earnestly and so repeatedly sought to avoid the calamities of war, by every decent method which wisdom could invent. Neither have I so much of the infidel in me, as to suppose that He has relinquished the government of the world, and given us up to the care of devils; and as I do not, I cannot see on what ground the king of Britain can look up to heaven for help against us: a common murderer, a highwayman, or a housebreaker, has as good a pretense as he... I am as confident, as I am that God governs the world, that America will never be happy till she gets clear of foreign dominion. Wars, without ceasing, will break out till that period arrives, and the continent must in the end be conqueror; for though the flame of liberty may sometimes cease to shine, the coal can never expire..."⁹

Like Gideon's 300, and the Pilgrim's 47, a small band of American patriots crossed the icy Delaware in a cruel winter storm on Christmas Eve of 1776. Their only casualties were two men who froze to death. These few--2600--turned the tide when all had seemed lost.

No "...summer soldiers or sunshine patriots!..." they laid their lives on the line to obtain the liberty the signers of the Declaration of Independence had proclaimed on July 4, 1776.

Signers of the Declaration of Independence.

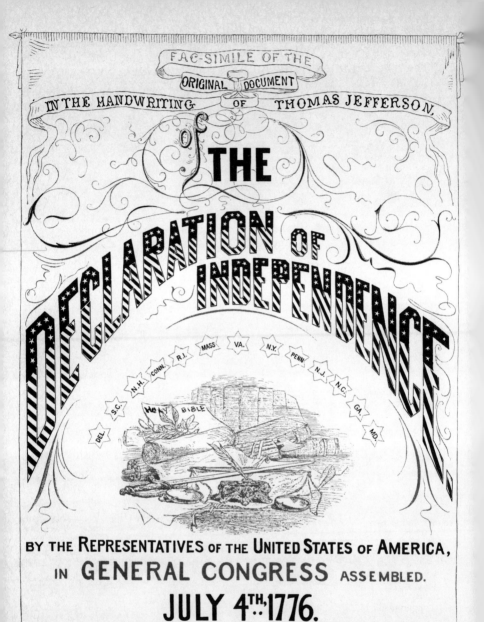

Declaration of Independence.

A Declaration by the Representatives of the UNITED STATES OF AMERICA. in General Congress assembled

When in the course of human events it becomes necessary for one people to dissolve the political bands which have connected them with another, and to ~~assume among them the~~ as -sume among the powers of the earth the separate and equal ~~equal & independent~~ station to which the laws of nature & of nature's god entitle them, a decent respect to the opinions of mankind requires that they should declare the causes which impel them to ~~the change~~ the separation.

We hold these truths to be self-evident; ~~sacred & undeniable~~; that all men are created equal ~~& independent~~; that ~~from that equal creation they derive~~ they are endowed by their creator with equal ~~rights~~ ~~inherent~~ ~~certain~~ inalienable rights; that among ~~which~~ these are ~~the preservation of~~ life & liberty, & the pursuit of happiness; that to secure these rights, go- -vernments are instituted among men, deriving their just powers from

Declaration of Independence.

91

the consent of the governed; that whenever any form of government ~~shall~~ becomes destructive of these ends, it is the right of the people to alter or to abolish it, & to institute new government, laying it's foundation on such principles & organising it's powers in such form, as to them shall seem most likely to effect their safety & happiness: prudence indeed will dictate that governments long established should not be changed for light & transient causes: and accordingly all experience hath shewn that mankind are more disposed to suffer while evils are sufferable, than to right themselves by abolishing the forms to which they are accustomed but when a long train of abuses & usurpations [begun at a distinguished period &] pursuing invariably the same object, evinces a design to ~~subject~~ reduce them ^under absolute Despotism, ~~to arbitrary power~~, it is their right, it is their duty, to throw off such government & to provide new guards for their future security. such has been the patient sufferance of these colonies. & such is now the necessity which constrains them to [^alter expunge] their former systems of government. the history of ~~his~~ ^the present ~~majesty~~, ^*king of Great Britain is a history of [^repeated unremitting] injuries and usurpations. [among which, ^appears no solitary fact ~~to prove~~ to contradict the uniform tenor of the rest, [all of which ^but all have ^having] in direct object the establishment of an absolute tyranny over these states. to prove this, let facts be submitted to a candid world, [for the truth of which we pledge a faith yet unsullied by falsehood]

he has refused his assent to laws the most wholesome and necessary for the public good:

he has forbidden his governors to pass laws of immediate & pressing importance, unless suspended in their operation till his assent should be obtained, and when so suspended, he has ^utterly neglected ~~attend~~ to attend to them.

Declaration of Independence.

92

he has refused to pass other laws for the accomodation of large districts of people
unless those people would relinquish the right of representation, in the legislature, a right
inestimable to them & formidable to tyrants only:
he has called together legislative bodies at places unusual, uncomfortable, & distant from
the depository of their public records, for the sole purpose of fatiguing them into compliance
with his measures;
he has dissolved Representative houses repeatedly [& continually] for opposing with
manly firmness his invasions on the rights of the people:
~~~~~~~~~~, he has refused for a long ~~space of time~~ time after such Dissolutions* to cause others to be elected
whereby the legislative power, incapable of annihilation, have returned to
the people at large for their exercise, the state remaining in the mean time
exposed to all the dangers of invasion from without & convulsions within:
he has endeavored to prevent the population of these states; for that purpose
obstructing the laws for naturalization of foreigners; refusing to pass others
to encourage their migrations hither, & raising the conditions of new ap.
-propriations of lands:
he has [suffered] obstructed the administration of justice [totally to cease in some of these
~~states~~] refusing his assent to laws for establishing judiciary powers:
he has made [our] judges dependant on his will alone, for the tenure of their offices
the + & payment
and amount of their salaries:
he has erected a multitude of new offices [by a self-assumed power] & sent hi-
-ther swarms of officers to harrass our people & eat out their substance.
he has kept among us in times of peace, ~~~~~~~~~~~~~~ standing armies [& ships of war,] without ~~no~~ the consent of our Legislatures
he has affected to render the military, independent of & superior to the civil power:
he has combined with others to subject us to a jurisdiction foreign to our constitu-

Declaration of Independence.

93

tions and unacknoleged by our laws; giving his assent to their pretended acts of

& legislation, for quartering large bodies of armed troops among us; .

  for protecting them by a mock-trial from punishment for any murders

    ^which they should commit on the inhabitants of these states;

for cutting off our trade with all parts of the world;

for imposing taxes on us without our consent;

for depriving us of the benefits of trial by jury;
    in many cases

for transporting us beyond seas to be tried for pretended offences:
for abolishing the free system of English laws in a neighboring province, establishing therein an arbitrary government
and enlarging it's boundaries, so as to render it at once an example & fit instrument for introducing the same absolute
— rule into these colonies [states]:

    †abolishing our most ~~important~~ valuable Laws

  for taking away our charters, & altering fundamentally the forms of our government:
                                      ^

  for suspending our own legislatures & declaring themselves invested with power to

    legislate for us in all cases whatsoever.
                                  by declaring us out of his protection & waging war against us.
he has abdicated government here, [withdrawing his governors, & declaring us out

    of his allegiance & protection:]

he has plundered our seas, ravaged our coasts, burnt our towns & destroyed the

    lives of our people:
                                                  Scotch and other
he is at this time transporting large armies of foreign mercenaries to compleat

    the works of death desolation & tyranny, already begun with circumstances
              scarcely parallelled in the most barbarous ages and totally
    of cruelty, & perfidy unworthy the head of a civilized nation.
he has also endeavored to bring on the inhabitants of our frontiers the merciless Indian
        excited domestic insurrections amongst us and has

    savages, whose known rule of warfare is an undistinguished destruction of

    all ages, sexes, & conditions [of existence.]

he has incited treasonable insurrections of our fellow-citizens with the

      allurements of forfeiture & confiscation of our property.
he has waged cruel war against human nature itself, violating it's most sa

    -cred rights of life & liberty in the persons of a distant people who never of

    fended him, captivating & carrying them into slavery in another hemis

Declaration of Independence.

94

-where, or to incur miserable death in their transportation thither. this piratical warfare the opprobruem of infidel powers, is the warfare of the Christian king of Great Britain [determined to keep open a market where MEN should be bought & sold he has prostituted his negative for suppressing every legislative attempt to prohibit or to restrain this ~~determining take open a market where MEN should be bought & sold~~: execrable commerce: and that this assemblage of horrors might want no fact of dis' inquished due, he is now exciting those very people to rise in arms among us, and to purchase that liberty of which he has deprived them by murdering the people upon whom he also obtruded them: thus paying off former crimes committed against the liberties of one people, with crimes which he urges them to commit against the lives of another.]

in every stage of these oppressions we have petitioned for redress in the most humble terms: our repeated petitions have been answered ^only by repeated injuries. a prince whose character is thus marked by every act which may define a tyrant, is unfit to be the ruler of a ~~people~~ [who mean to be free] future ages will scarce believe that the hardiness of one man, adventured within the short compass of twelve years to ~~lay~~ ^build a foundation so broad & undisguised for tyranny only, ~~over so many acts of tyranny without a mask~~ over a people fostered & fixed in principles of ~~liberty~~, freedom]

Nor have we been wanting in attentions to our British brethren: we have warned them from time to time of attempts by their legislature to extend ^an unwarrantable a jurisdiction over [these our states]. we have reminded them of the circumstances of our emigration & settlement here, [no one of which could warrant so strange a pretension: that these were effected at the expence of our own blood & treasure, unassisted by the wealth or the strength of Great Britain: that in constituting indeed our several forms of government, we had adopted one common king, thereby laying a foundation for perpetual league & amity with them: but that submission to their parliament was no part of our constitution, nor ever in idea if history may be

Declaration of Independence.

credited: and we have appealed to their native justice & magnanimity [as well as to the ties
of our common kindred to disavow these usurpations which [were likely to] interrupt
our correspondence & connection &. they too have been deaf to the voice of justice &
of consanguinity. [& when occasions have been given them, by the regular course of
their laws, of removing from their councils the disturbers of our harmony, they
have by their free election re-established them in power. at this very time too they
are permitting their chief magistrate to send over not only soldiers of our common
blood, but Scotch & foreign mercenaries to invade & destroy us. these facts
have given the last stab to agonizing affection, and manly spirit bids us to re-
-nounce for ever these unfeeling brethren. we must endeavor to forget our former
love for them, and to hold them as we hold the rest of mankind, enemies in war,
in peace friends. we might have been a free & a great people together; but a commu-
-nication of grandeur & of freedom it seems is below their dignity. be it so, since they
will have it: the road to happiness is open to us too; we will tread it
apart from them, and acquiesce in the necessity which pronounces our
separation!

We therefore the representatives of the United States of America in General Congress assembled, do in the name & by authority of the good people of these [states]
[reject and renounce all allegiance & subjection to the kings of Great Britain
& all others who may hereafter claim by, through, or under them; we utterly
dissolve all political connection which may heretofore have sub-
-sisted between us & the people or parliament of Great Britain; and finally
we do assert and declare these colonies to be free and independant states,
and that as free & independant states they have full power to levy
war conclude peace, contract alliances, establish commerce, & to do all other
acts and things which independant states may of right do. and for the
support of this declaration] we mutually pledge to each other our lives, our
fortunes & our sacred honour.

Declaration of Independence.

John Penn John Hancock John Hart

Wm Floyd Wm Paca

Geo Read Wm Hooper Sam Adams

Step Hopkins Tho Nelson jr Geo Clymer

Tho M: Kean Charles Carroll of Carrollton Elbridge Gerry

Roger Sherman Sam el Huntington

Wm Whipple Thomas Lynch Jun r

Geo Taylor Josiah Bartlett Benj Franklin

Wm Williams Rich d Stockton

John Morton

Oliver Wolcott Jno Witherspoon Geo. Ross

Tho Stone Samuel Chase Rob t Treat Paine

George Wythe Matthew Thornton

Fran s Lewis Th Jefferson Benj a Harrison

Lewis Morris Abra Clark Phil Livingston

Casar Rodney

Arthur Middleton Fra s Hopkinson

Geo Walton Carter Braxton James Wilson

Richard Henry Lee Tho s Heyward Jun r

Benjamin Rush John Adams Rob Morris

Lyman Hall Joseph Hewes Button Gwinnett

Francis Lightfoot Lee

William Ellery Edward Rutledge Ja s Smith

Declaration of Independence.

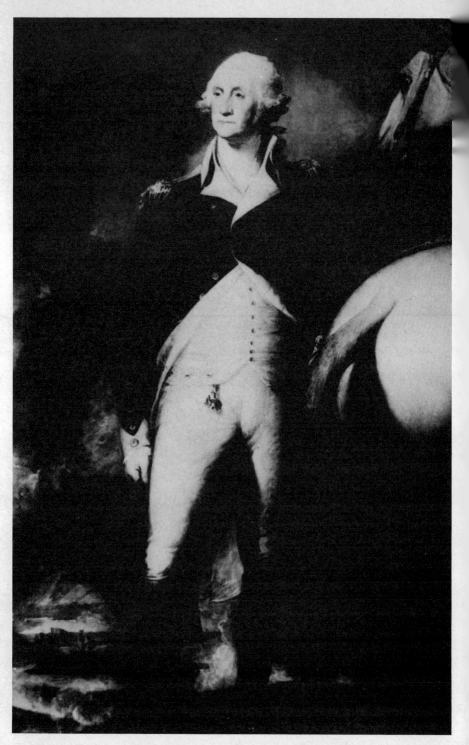

George Washington at Dorchester Heights
by Gilbert Stuart, National Archives

George Washington's Birthday-- The Father Of Our Country

CHAPTER ONE

The Education of George Washington

Why would a noted modern historian say of George Washington, "No doubt at all he, personally, was ninety percent of the force which made of the American Revolution a successful issue. Know of what that force consisted...that is, Washington himself, and you will know practically all there is to understand about the beginnings of the American republic...?"[1]

What caused another modern historian to entitle his biography, *Washington, The Indispensable Man*?[2]

Why was he selected Commander-in-Chief of the Continental army even before The Declaration of Independence and elected our first president for two terms with no opposition?

Why could his enemies--the Indians in the French and Indian War and the British in the War for Independence--find no fault in him? Why was he deified by the Indians who fought him in the French and Indian War and offered a crown by the soldiers who served with him in the Revolutionary War? And why did he reject it so vehemently?

How was he able to win the war against the mightiest nation in the world when that nation had such strong support from loyalists within the colonies themselves while he never had adequate logistical forces or support from the Continental Congress and never could count on adequate replacement of men or supplies?

And then there was that statement by his wife, Martha, which should put him in *The Guinness Book of Records,* "George is right. He is always right!"[3]

I found only one explanation, and Washington gave it over and over by his words and in his life. This remarkable man who constantly invoked and thanked God for His divine providence actually was under God's divine providence!

A contemporary of Washington said it well in a biographical sketch, "When the children of the years to come, hearing his great name reechoed from every lip, shall say to their fathers, 'What was it that raised Washington to such heights of glory?' let them be told that it was GREAT TALENTS CONSTANTLY GUIDED AND GUARDED BY RELIGION...the noblest, the most efficient element of his character was that he was an humble, earnest Christian."[4]

I was never told that! Were you? Instead I found many apparent attempts to conceal this secret of his greatness, many blatant lies to defame his character--all of which have been disproved by careful historians. One highly respected modern biographer concluded, "Those who have had the pleasure of working on the life of Washington, have, through the years, seen one falsehood after another proven to be totally without foundation...Our superb national heritage is founded on the life and conduct of a truly great, and totally honest man."[5]

Abraham Lincoln wrote of him, "Washington is the mightiest name on earth--long since mightiest in the cause of civil liberty, still mightiest in moral reformation...To add brightness to the sun, or glory to the name of Washington is alike impossible. Let none attempt it. In solemn awe we pronounce the name and in its naked splendor leave it shining on."[6]

In spite of the many denials of George Washington's being a Christian, the historical evidence provided in forty volumes of his diary, letters, orders to the army, addresses, and state papers, supply irrefutable evidence of his lifelong faith in God and His Son, Jesus Christ, and consistent obedience to His Word, *The Bible*. Then there is the consistent affirmation of his Christian contemporaries. In the light of the overwhelming evidence, it is intellectually untenable for anyone to deny he was a Christian.

There was Washington's heritage of faith from his great-great grandfather, a clergyman in the Church of England; and from his great grandfather, who came to Virginia in 1657 and founded a parish which was called for him, "The Parish of Washington."

He willed the church a tablet with the Ten Commandments, and wrote, "...being heartily sorry from the bottom of my heart for my sins past, most humbly desiring forgiveness of the same from the Almighty God my Saviour and redeemer in whom and by the merits of Jesus Christ, I trust and believe assuredly to be saved, and to have full remission and forgiveness of all my sins."

This faith was also expressed in the will of his grandfather, and his father, who was a vestryman in Trudo Parish. George Washington was not only a fourth generation American, he was a fourth generation American Christian.[7]

His mother's family were equally faithful churchmen. His great grandfather Warner left the church a silver communion service, and his uncle led a movement to educate church ministers.[8]

Love of the church was George Washington's strong inheritance, and he affirmed it with habitual attendance at church and by humbly accepting religious instruction from his mother, who described his essential characteristic as teachable.

One of the books from which she taught him was *Contemplations: Moral and Divine,* by Sir Matthew Hale. It was found in the library of Mt. Vernon after Washington died, and had many pencil marks attesting to his choice and study of many of its passages. Washington Irving, in his *Life of Washington,* 1857, wrote of this book, "Let those who wish to know the moral foundation of his character consult its pages."[9]

"As a boy he learned with remarkable rapidity because he was an attentive, disciplined pupil; he had a pronounced characteristic of *teachableness,"* wrote one biographer. "Washington's willingness to listen to others was a very important element in carrying the Constitutional Convention through a long, hot summer to brilliant success."[10]

When George was eleven his father died, ending the education he was giving him and not leaving enough money for him to study abroad as had his father and two older stepbrothers. George seemed to have no resentment, for two years later he copied in a folio 110 maxims entitled, "Rules of Civility," the 108th rule of which said, "When you speak of God or His attributes, let it be Seriously and (with words of) Reverence, Honor and Obey your natural parents though they be poor..."[11]

Although deprived of a formal education, he not only was taught by his father and two stepbrothers who were all educated at Appleby Grammar School in England, but came under the influence of his neighbor, Colonel William Fairfax, who treated him as a member of his family, gave him access to his library--the best in the country--and shared with George the education he had. It happened to be the best that England could provide, including his experiences in the British Navy through which he had seen much of the world.

When George Washington was fifteen he began to learn the much-needed occupation of land surveyor and when he was sixteen Colonel Fairfax employed him to survey his extensive holdings over the frontier of the Blue Ridge mountains in the Shenandoah Valley.

From that time on he supported himself very well and made excellent investments in land. Everywhere he went people were impressed by this tall, dignified, aristocratic young man who had so much wisdom.

At the early age of fifteen years he was chosen as a godfather, and again at sixteen and twenty-eight. When he was 20 years old, he went to Barbados in the West Indies with his beloved older brother, Lawrence, who was terminally ill with tuberculosis.[12]

His journal showed he attended church while there, but the most irrefutable proof that he was a Christian is shown in a pocket memo book he kept entitled *Daily Sacrifices*. It contains in his handwriting prayers for morning and evening, Sunday through Thursday. The fate of the Friday through Saturday devotionals is not known, but what was retained in this little book was recorded in *Washington's Barbados Journal, 1751-2* by J. M. Toner and sold at an auction which was held April 21 through 23, 1891 in Philadelphia.[13]

Professor S. F. Uphan, professor of practical theology at Drew Theological Seminary wrote, "The daily prayers of George Washington abound in earnest thought, expressed in simple, beautiful, fervent and evangelical language. They reveal to us the real life of the great patriot, and attest his piety...The prayers are characterized by a deep consciousness of sin and by a need of forgiveness, and by a recognition of dependence upon the merits and mercies of our Lord. They contain fervent applications for family, friends, and rulers in church and state."[14]

Let those who call him a deist consider these words from the first of those daily prayers:

"...since thou art a God of pure eyes, and wilt be sanctified in all who draw near unto thee, who doest not regard the sacrifice of fools, nor hear sinners who tread in thy courts, pardon, I beseech thee, my sins, remove them from thy presence, as far as the east is from the west, and accept of me for the merits of thy son Jesus Christ, that when I come into thy temple and compass thine altar, my prayer may come before thee as incense; and as thou wouldst hear me calling upon thee in my prayer, so give me grace to hear thee calling on me in thy word, that it may be wisdom, righteousness, reconciliation and peace to the saving of my soul in the day of the Lord Jesus. Grant that I may hear it with reverence, receive it with meekness, mingle it with faith, and that it may accomplish in me, Gracious God, the good work for which thou has sent it. Bless my family, kindred, friends and country, be our God and guide this day and for ever for his sake, who lay down in the Grave and arose again for us, Jesus Christ our Lord. Amen."

His Sunday evening prayer included, "...remit my transgressions, negligences and ignorances, and cover them all with the absolute obedience of thy dear Son, that those sacrifices which I have offered may be accepted by thee, in and for the sacrifice of Jesus Christ offered upon the cross for me; for his sake, ease me of the burden of my sins, and give me grace that by the call of the Gospel I may rise from the slumber of sin in the newness of life...open the eyes of my understanding, and help me thoroughly to examine myself concerning my knowledge, faith and repentance, increase my faith, and direct me to the true object Jesus Christ, the way,the truth and the life...for the sake of thy Dear Son Jesus Christ our Lord. Amen."

In his Monday evening prayer he wrote, "...Thou mad'st me at first and hast ever since sustained the work of thy own hand; thou gav'st thy Son to die for me; and hast given me assurance of salvation, upon my repentance and sincerely endeavoring to conform my life to his holy precepts and example...let the whole world be filled with the knowledge of Thee and thy son Jesus Christ..."[15]

These prayers were written when he was 20 years of age. From that time onward, if any American has demonstrated the fact that Christianity is the basis of his character and greatness, in my opinion, George Washington was that man.

Upon returning from Barbados, he was commissioned to bear dispatches to the French Commander, St. Pierre. When he bade farewell to his mother, she told him, "...remember that God only is our sure trust. To Him I commend you." As he turned to leave, she warned him, "My son, neglect not the duty of secret prayer."[16]

He not only prayed secretly, but also led public prayers at Fort Necessity, where the participants were poorly equipped soldiers and painted Indians with their wives and children. Here he began an acknowledgment of divine Providence which he continued throughout his life: "...we should have been six days without provisions, if Providence had not sent a trader from Ohio to our relief..."[17]

Later, when offered an important command during the French and Indian War, his mother objected. He replied, "The God to whom you commended me, madam, when I set out upon a more perilous errand, defended me from all harm, and I trust he will do so now. Do not you?"[18]

His commanding general, Braddock, was mortally wounded in the battle of the Monongahela. The chaplain having been wounded, Washington read the funeral service by the light of a torch, risking the threat of an Indian attack to give him a Christian burial.

Five days later, he wrote to his brother, John, (who had been told he was killed in action,) "...by the all-powerful dispensations of Providence, I have been protected beyond all human probability or expectation; for I had four bullets through my coat, and two horses shot under me, yet escaped unhurt, although death was leveling my companions on every side of me!"[19]

It seems he was not alone in his amazement and assurance of God's protection of him from gunfire on that and future occasions.

In 1818, the following testimony of an Indian Chief was given the grandson of Martha Washington, George Washington Park Curtis, as told by an eyewitness, and published in his *Recollections and Private Memoirs of Washington* in 1860:

"Fifteen years after this battle Washington and Dr. Craig, his intimate friend from his boyhood to his death, were traveling on an expedition to the western country, for the purpose of exploring wild lands. While near the junction of the Great Kanawha and Ohio Rivers, a company of Indians came to them with an interpreter, at the head of whom was an aged and venerable chief. The council fire was kindled, when the chief addressed Washington through an interpreter to the following effect:

"I am a chief, and ruler over my tribes. My influence extends to the waters of the great lakes, and to the far blue mountains. I have traveled a long and weary path that I might see the young warrior of the great battle. It was on the day when the white man's blood mixed with the streams of our forest, that I first beheld this chief. I called to my young men and said, Mark yon tall and daring warrior? He is not of the red-coat tribe--he hath an Indian's wisdom, and his warriors fight as we do--himself is alone exposed. Quick, let your aim be certain, and he dies. Our rifles were leveled, rifles which, but for him, knew not how to miss--'twas all in vain, a power mightier far than we shielded him from harm. He cannot die in battle. I am old, and soon shall be gathered to the great council fire of my fathers in the land of shades, but ere I go, there is something bids me speak in the voice of prophecy. Listen! *The Great Spirit protects that man, and guides his destinies--he will become the chief of nations, and a people yet unborn will hail him as the founder of a mighty empire."* [20]

Described by George Mercer, his close friend, as "...straight as an Indian...wide shouldered...long arms and legs. His neck is well shaped...gracefully poised on a superb neck. A large and straight, rather than prominent nose, bluegrey penetrating eyes which are widely separated and overhung by a heavy brow. His face is long rather than broad...and terminates in a good firm chin. He has a clear skin which burns with the sun. A pleasant, benevolent, commanding countenance, dark brown hair, which he wears in a cue. His mouth is large and generally firmly closed.

His features are regular and placid, with all the muscles of his face under perfect control...In conversation he looks you full in the face, is deliberate, differential, and engaging. His voice is agreeable rather than strong. His movements and gestures are graceful."

Further described as devoid of ostentation, wise, philanthropic, magnanimous, thoughtful but never worried, enjoying a humorous observation and making them himself, and sometimes laughing heartily, this animated young man with the lively blue eyes, although weighing between 215 and 225 pounds always stood to his 6'3" height and was perceived as sparse, lean, powerful. Little wonder he found favor everywhere he went.[21]

While other young men of his acquaintance were going abroad to obtain an education, he was learning from his father, his stepbrothers, and his learned neighbor Colonel Fairfax and his superb library, and in the school of hard knocks as a surveyor and soldier in the wilderness. It is significant that Professor Albert Bushnell Hart of Harvard University stated, "George Washington was the best educated man of his time."[22]

Crossing the Delaware, by Emanuel Leutze, National Archives

CHAPTER TWO

With A Firm Reliance
On The Providence of God

George Washington, now 21 years old, returned from the dangerous assignment Governor Dinwiddie had sent him on branded incompetent by the British and a hero by the Virginians. But he had gained what was to be a lifelong trust in the providence of God.

Denied his commission of Colonel and reduced in rank because no provincial was to be allowed a rank higher than captain, he resigned from the army the following year. Later, he was recalled and made commander of the Virginia militia. By the time the French and Indian War was over he had become the most experienced and best qualified military leader among the colonials. His officers, many of whom were older than he, wrote a letter, thanking him for his impartial justice, and concluding, "In you we place the most implicit confidence. Your presence is all that is needed to cause a steady firmness and vigor to actuate in every breast, despising the greatest dangers and thinking light of toils and hardships; while led on by the man we know and love."[1]

With the French and Indian War behind him, he married a wealthy young widow, Martha Curtis, on January 6, 1759. Together with his inheritance of Mt. Vernon from his brother, Lawrence, and the astute investments he had made in the Shenandoah Valley as a land surveyor, he became one of the richest men in the colonies.

A successful farmer, the most respected military man in his country, a member of the House of Burgesses, and a responsible churchman, he also loved fox-hunting and entertaining. (Fox-hunting was necessary to save the farmers from a voracious fox population as well as being hearty recreation for the fun-loving Virginia planters.)

Fortunately for us, George Washington was blessed with a wife who also trusted in God and in him. In 1774, when the trouble with England was growing, Martha Washington wrote to a kinswoman, "Yes, I foresee consequences--dark days, domestic happiness suspended, social enjoyments abandoned, and eternal separation on earth possible. But my mind is made up, my heart is in the cause. George is right; he is always right. God has promised to protect the righteous, and I will trust Him."[2]

Always the patriot, Washington helped form the Committees of Correspondence and wrote his friend, George Mason, "...at a time when our lordly masters in Great Britain will be satisfied with nothing less than the deprivation of American freedom, something must be done to avert the stroke and maintain the liberty which we have derived from our ancestors..."

Desiring peace, but not at the price of liberty, he added, "That no man should scruple to or hesitate a moment to use arms in defense of so valuable a blessing is clearly my opinion. Yet arms...should be the last resort..."

He then proposed non-importation measures, which he and Mason had discussed, and lived up to them rigidly. Neither tea or any of the proscribed articles were allowed in his house because he realized the colonies were now trying the last peaceful remedy, and that the next step would be war.

When the Boston Tea Party was followed by the closing of Boston Harbour, the Virginia legislature met at the Raleigh Tavern--because of the British dissolution of the Assembly--and appointed a day of fasting, humiliation and prayer on June 1, 1775. On the first of June, 1775, Washington's diary showed he fasted all day and attended the appointed prayer services.

They held another meeting where the Boston Bill was denounced, non-importation renewed, and the Committee of Correspondence instructed to call a general congress.

To his British friend and neighbor, Bryan Fairfax, who remonstrated with him, he wrote, "Does it not appear clear as the sun in its meridian brightness that there is a regular systematic plan formed to fix the right and practice of taxation on us? Does not the uniform conduct of Parliament for some years confirm this?...Is not the attack upon the liberty and property of the people of Boston, before restitution of the loss to the India Company was demanded, a plain and self-evident proof of what they are aiming at? Do not the subsequent bills (now I dare say acts) for depriving the Massachusetts Bay of its charter and for transporting offenders into other colonies, or to Great Britain for trial, where it is impossible from the nature of the thing that justice be obtained, convince us that the administration is determined to stick at nothing to carry its point? Ought we not, then to put our virtue and fortitude to the severest test?"[3]

They met that test when, on April 19, 1775 , the British Commander at Boston sent a force of 700 redcoats to Concord to destroy the American Patriots' supply depot. Warned by Paul Revere and William Dawes, this "secret mission" was met at Lexington by militiamen, whose Captain Parker ordered, "Don't fire unless fired upon, but if they mean to have war, let it begin here."

When Washington learned the British had fired "...the shot heard 'round the world," and that several Americans had been killed at Lexington, he said, "I grieve for the death of my countrymen, but rejoice that the British are still determined to keep God on our side."

Later he explained, "The smiles of Heaven can never be expected on a nation that disregards the eternal rules of order and right, which Heaven itself has ordained."[4]

Upon being appointed commander of the Colonial Army, Washington wrote his wife, "I shall rely, therefore, confidently on that Providence, which has heretofore preserved and been bountiful to me, not doubting but that I shall return safe to you in the fall." (It was to be six long difficult years before he returned to his beloved Mt. Vernon home, but his reliance on divine providence never faltered. God is not on our timetable!) Four days later, June 22, he wrote her, "I go, fully trusting in that Providence which has been more bountiful than I deserve."

On July 4, 1775, the day after he took command of the Continental Army, he issued an order stating, "The General most earnestly requires and expects a due observance of those articles of war established for the government of the army, which forbid profane cursing, swearing, and drunkenness. And in like manner he requires and expects of all officers and soldiers not engaged in actual duty, a punctual attendance on Divine service, to implore the blessing of Heaven upon the means used for our safety and defense."[5]

Chaplain William Emerson wrote a friend that "New orders from his excellency are read to the respective regiments every morning, after prayers."[6]

July 20, 1775 was selected a day of fasting and prayer throughout the colonies. The pastors, who had tremendous influence on the people, prepared them through sermons which were also printed and passed around. Convinced of the importance of repentance and prayer if they were to carry through to a successful conclusion this unequal contest upon which they were entering and realizing everything dear to them was in jeopardy, their pastors reminded them of God's providence to their forefathers as they settled this country, and of the fact that they were not without hope.

Washington arrived at Boston shortly after the Battle of Bunker Hill, which was being won by the Colonials...until they ran out of ammunition and were forced to retreat.

On January 14, 1776, he wrote Joseph Reed concerning the difficulties of obtaining food, clothing, guns, etc:

"...Few people know the predicament we are in on a thousand accounts...if instead of taking the command under such circumstances, I had taken my musket on my shoulder and entered the ranks, or, if I could have justified the measure to posterity and my own conscience, have retired to the back country and lived in a wigwam...If I shall be able to rise superior to these and many other difficulties which might be enumerated, I shall most religiously believe that the finger of Providence is in it, to blind the eyes of our enemies; for surely if we get through this month, it must be for want of their knowing the disadvantages we labor under."[7]

They did get through that month and many others. And on March 6. he issued the following order: "Thursday, the 7th instant, being set apart by the honorable Legislature of this Province as a day of fasting, prayer, and humiliation...to implore the Lord and Giver of all victory to pardon our manifold sins and wickedness, and that it would please Him to bless the Continental army with His divine favor and protection."[8]

Always short of guns and ammunition, they remembered the fifty British guns at Fort Ticonderoga which had been captured without a shot being fired at the beginning of the war. The guns were still there, and Washington desperately needed them.

The problem was how to get more than fifty tons of guns over the muddy, icy roads to Boston. But it was no problem to a heavy-weight twenty-five-year-old American amateur engineer. Sleds! And God supplied the snow![9]

On the evening of March 4, 1776, 800 of Washington's soldiers had silently moved into Dorchester Heights and, the ground being frozen so they could not dig trenches, made ramparts (called chandeliers) according to plans in a French textbook on warfare one of his young officers "just happened to stumble on." Adding a purely American touch, they had filled barrels with stones and placed them in front of the chandeliers.

Viewing the ramparts the next morning, a British army engineer officer, Captain Charles Stuart, said, "..a most astonishing night's work that must have employed from 15,000 to 20,000 men!" Captain Charles Stuart wrote the fortifications "...appeared more like magic than the work of human beings!" British General Howe had to admit, "The rebels have done more in one night than my whole army would have done in months!"[10]

The miracle was the British in Boston were caught totally by surprise. A ground mist perfectly concealed the colonials' activities from the base of Dorchester Heights where the British were, while the weather at the top where the colonials were working was perfectly clear. And, wonder of wonders, nothing went wrong to warn the British.

The next morning, to save face, Howe ordered 2000 of his forces to embark on the next tide--but, as they waited for the tide, a storm of nearly hurricane violence made amphibious operations impossible. It continued all night, and Howe decided a frontal attack was now impossible. When Washington took over Nob

Hill, the British realized their position was untenable and abruptly evacuated the city they had held for a year and a half.[11]

Eleven days after the day of fasting and prayer, without a single loss of life, the British evacuated Boston! Within hours after their departure a Thanksgiving service was held at the request of General Washington. He and his officers heard the minister preach from Exodus 14:25: "...the Egyptians said, Let us flee from the face of Israel; for the Lord fighteth for them against the Egyptians." And indeed to many it was becoming clear the Lord was fighting for the Americans against the British![12]

A few days later the leaders of Boston, the Clergy, and many other Gentlemen, met at the Council Chamber and proceeded to the old Brick Meeting House where a sermon on Isaiah 33:20 was delivered. (No separation of church and state that day!) Afterward they celebrated with an elegant dinner at the *Bunch of Grapes Tavern*. The April 9, 1776 issue of the *Boston Post* reported, "Joy and gratitude sat on every countenance, and smiled in every eye."[13]

Washington wrote his brother, Austin, concerning the evacuation of Boston, "...great preparations were made for attacking them; but not being ready before the afternoon, and the weather getting very tempestuous, much blood was saved, and a very important blow, to one side or the other, was prevented. That this most remarkable interposition of Providence is for some wise purpose, I have not a doubt.

"I have been here months together with what will scarcely be believed--not thirty rounds of musket cartridges a man. We have maintained our ground against their army...we have disbanded one army and recruited another within musket shot of two and twenty regiments, the flower of the British army, and at last have beat them, in a shameful and precipitate manner out of a place the strongest by nature on this continent..."[14]

Actually, his triumphant army had not yet met the enemy in battle! Instead, it had been saved from what would have probably been a terrible and costly defeat! And that defeat at that time might have meant the end of the Revolution!

Washington did respond to an address from the General Assembly of Massachusetts, following the British evacuation of Boston by acknowledging "...it being effected without the blood of our soldiers and fellow-citizens must be ascribed to the interposition of that Providence which has manifestly appeared on our behalf through the whole of this important struggle, as well as to the measures pursued for bringing about the happy event...

"May that Being who is powerful to save, and in whose hands is the fate of nations, look down with an eye of tender pity; and compassion upon the whole of the United Colonies; may He continue to smile upon their counsels and arms, and crown them with success, whilst employed in the cause of virtue and mankind. May this distressed colony and its capital, and every part of this wide extended continent, through His divine favor, be restored to more than their former lustre and once happy state, and have peace, liberty, and safety secured upon a solid, permanent and lasting foundation."[15]

Washington Praying at Valley Forge

CHAPTER THREE

Forged in the Valleys

The British had fled from Boston to New York by way of Halifax where they refitted their hastily loaded ships. At the insistence of the Continental Congress the American army preceded them by two months although Washington was fully aware of the odds against him.

On July 6, he received a copy of *The Declaration of Independence* and had it read to his troops, who greeted it with cheers.

In the face of an expected attack from the British, he told his men: "The time is now at hand which must probably determine whether Americans are to be freemen or slaves; whether they are to have any property they can call their own; whether their houses and farms are to be pillaged and destroyed, and they consigned to a state of wretchedness, from which no human efforts will probably deliver them...The fate of unborn millions will now depend, under God, on the courage and conduct of this army...Our cruel and unrelenting enemy leaves us no choice but brave resistance or the most abject submission...if we now shamefully fail, we shall become infamous to the whole world. Let us rely upon the goodness of the cause, and the aid of the Supreme Being in whose hands victory is, to animate and encourage us to great and noble actions..."[1]

He wrote his brother of the unpreparedness of the army for the task before it, but added, "However, it is to be hoped that, if our cause is just, as I do most religiously believe it to be, the same Providence, which has in many instances appeared for us, will still go on to afford its aid."[2]

Greatly outnumbered and outmaneuvered, the Americans marveled at the failure of the British land troops to attack when they had the Americans cornered at the East River! They were amazed

117

at Howe's delay until a northeast wind prevented his fleet entering the East River! Historians have long affirmed that Howe threw away a great opportunity while Washington's own men were in great fear and confusion. Three days later, Howe, who was certain he had the American force trapped on the shore of Long Island, woke up to find the entire army of 9000 men had been moved across a strait of strong tides and currents 3/4 mile in width in boats their volunteers, good fishermen, had gathered from a distance. A providential fog had concealed their activities from the British until the last boat had left with Washington on it. And all of it had taken place within sight and hearing of the British, who had fought a successful battle and were sure they had the Americans in their grasp! It was a miraculous evacuation reminiscent of Dunkirk in the Second World War. One wonders if the prayers of Rev. Duche at the first meeting of the First Continental Congress, now so wonderfully answered, were recalled at this time.

"As the dawn approached, those of us who remained became very anxious for our own safety," wrote Major Ben Tallmadge. "At this time a very dense fog began to rise, and it seemed to settle in a peculiar manner over both encampments. I recollect this peculiar providential occurrence perfectly well, and so very dense was the atmosphere that I could scarcely discern a man at six yards distance...we tarried until the sun had risen, but the fog remained as dense as ever."[3]

That fog was there until the last boat with Washington in it had departed. When it lifted, the surprised and shocked British ran to the shore and started firing after them, but the Americans were out of range.

Thanks to the providence of God in sending too many "coincidences" to number, the Continental Army had survived and not one soldier had been lost!

Again, the British allowed Washington's troops time to recover before crossing to Manhattan because, as one British critic said, "Howe calculated with the greatest accuracy the exact time necessary to allow his enemy to escape." First, he waited two full weeks before crossing to Manhattan, giving the Americans time to recuperate, resupply and reposition themselves. Then he remained at the home of Mrs. Robert Murray, enjoying her company, cake, and madiera wine, and giving the American army two precious hours.

"The tarrying of Howe at the home of Mrs. Robert Murray, a Quaker, who was secretly a friend of the American cause, saved this part of the America Army," said Dr.James Thatcher,surgeon of the Continental Army.[4]

It was surely a miracle that Washington had been able to extricate his forces from a situation Congress had urged him to hold at all cost--a position where every probability pointed to defeat, followed by almost certain capture or destruction.

In the dark days of the war, he wrote his brother, "No man, I believe, ever had a greater choice of difficulties, and less means to extricate himself from them. However, under full persuasion of the justice of our cause, I cannot entertain an idea that it will finally sink, though it may remain for some time under a cloud."[5]

No complaint, no boasting, no despair, no bitterness in reference to Congress's failure to supply his army, and to the officer who disobeyed his order and surrendered to the British instead of coming to his aid. Instead, he not only wrote strongly, but he pledged his own estate and exceeded his powers in desperate efforts to raise money and men, writing Congress on December 20, 1776, "A character to lose, an estate to forfeit, the inestimable blessings of liberty at stake, and a life devoted, must be my excuse."[6]

King George III had experienced the greatest difficulty in raising an army, because of widespread sympathy for the American cause.

William Pitt, the foremost British statesman of the eighteenth century said, "The spirit which now resists your taxation in America is the same which formerly...established the great fundamental, essential maxim of your liberties-- that no subject of England shall be taxed but by his own consent. This glorious spirit...animates three millions in America, who prefer poverty with liberty, to gilded chains and sordid affluence, and who will die in deference of their rights as men, as freemen.

"When your lordships look at the papers transmitted us from America, when you consider their decency, firmness and wisdom, you cannot but respect their cause, and wish to make it your own.

For myself, I must declare and avow...no nation or body of men can stand in preference to the general Congress at Philadelphia."

The Bishop of Saint Asalph addressed the Parliament, "My Lords, I look upon North America as the only great nursery of freedom now left on the face of the earth...we seem not to be sensible of the high and important trust which Providence has committed to our charge. The most precious remains of civil liberty that the world can now boast of are lodged in our hands, and God forbid that we should violate so sacred a deposit."[7]

The Lord Mayor and Aldermen of London petitioned the King, "We are persuaded that, by the sacred, unalterable rights of human nature, as well as by every principle of the constitution, the Americans ought to enjoy peace, liberty and safety, and that whatever power invades these rights ought to be resisted. We hold such resistance, in vindication of their constitutional rights, to be their indispensable duty to God, from whom those rights are derived to themselves."[8]

All of England, Scotland, and Ireland felt strongly about America's fate. The highest officers in the army and navy refused to serve and openly opposed the war. Never in all British history had she experienced such trouble raising an army. Her recruiters were stoned in Ireland and tarred and feathered in Wales. But, as many sermons pointed out, like Pharaoh, King George's heart was hardened and he refused to listen.[9]

Finally, he was forced to hire mercenaries abroad, but Catherine of Russia did not reply to his hand-written request, and Frederick the Great curtly refused him. Holland's leader told his people he thought "...the Americans worthy of every man's esteem ...a brave people, defending in a becoming, manly and religious manner those rights which, as men, they derive from God, not from the legislature of Great Britain."[10]

He was able to get thirty thousand German mercenaries from the lesser princes of Germany who, as Edmund Burke said, "...sniffed the cadaverous taint of lucrative war." These hired German soldiers made up half of the British force in America.[11]

On Christmas Eve, 1776, while the western world was rejoicing and feasting, and the British and Hessian soldiers in New

York and New Jersey were reveling and drinking, Washington crossed the Delaware in a bitter snow and hailstorm which kept the British sentries inside. They fought a predawn battle that saved the Revolution with less than 6000 men, only 2400 of whom participated.

The Hessian garrison was completely surprised. "The hurry, fright and confusion of the enemy was not unlike that which will be when the last trump will sound," wrote Henry Knox.[12]

Washington lost two men who were frozen to death on the march, and three were wounded. They took almost a thousand prisoners in forty-five minutes of fighting.

Cornwallis was ordered to Trenton, which he reached on January 2 with heavy reinforcements. Against the advice of his officers who warned against delay, he said he could just as well "bag the fox" the next morning. But "the fox" slipped away in the night, leaving his campfires burning, and not only drove back a column of soldiers on their way to join Cornwallis, but captured Princeton.[13]

The tide had been turned!

Frederick the Great is reported to have said this was the most brilliant campaign of the century. Certainly, these amazing successes revived the patriotic spirit of the colonials, and gave fresh hope and courage to the whole country.

From that time on the 13 states had great faith in Washington. One British traveller reported, "Volunteer companies are collecting in every county on the continent, and in a few months the rascals will be stronger than ever. Even the parsons, some of them, have turned out as volunteers and pulpits drum--or thunder, which you please to call it--summoning all to arms in this cursed babble."[14]

But Washington never had enough men to launch a major offensive. In addition he had to allow it to be supposed that he had more troops than he had and so the congress, complaining that he did not do more and fight more battles, made unending trouble for him. In addition, there were ambitious officers who complained to the congress which was no longer composed of the men who had commissioned Washington. Men like Franklin, Adams, John Jay, Hancock, and others were needed elsewhere and had been replaced by lesser men who lacked their wisdom.

Ft. Ticonderoga was lost on July 8. 1777. While British General Burgoyne and seven thousand men were captured at Saratoga the following October in the greatest victory of the war, the Continental Army had been badly hurt at Brandywine trying in vain to prevent the British taking Philadelphia. America's chief city, from which liberty had been proclaimed, was now a British armed camp, liberty and independence were a fading dream, and the question was how long America could endure.[15]

Worse, Washington's army was now threatened with a more powerful enemy--his men were exhausted, hungry, half naked, and freezing. Of the 11,000 men who stumbled into Valley Forge on December 19, 1977, less than a dozen were equipped for the cruel winter that awaited them. Silently, they filed past Washington, who could only encourage them with the fact that he was there. But it was in the agony of Valley Forge that an army was tempered that would stand in spite of whatever dangers they faced--an army that would confound the British.

Meanwhile, holed up in comfortable quarters in Philadelphia, the British turned a church into a riding academy for the cavalry, burning the pews and pulpit for fuel and putting a grog shop in the gallery. (More than fifty non-Anglican churches were totally destroyed, and dozens of others damaged or abused during the war.)[16]

At the same time, ministers across America began to sense the spiritual struggle that was being waged at Valley Forge, and they were comparing Washington to Moses, who "...chose to suffer with the people of God..." They saw that while the British were offending God and man in Philadelphia, Washington and his men, encamped fifteen miles away at Valley Forge, were suffering hunger and many were barefooted and freezing.

It was an early and cruelly cold winter, and the army worked desperately to build the 700 log cabins they needed before they froze to death. It was done in less than a month and only after the last man was quartered did Washington leave his own leaky tent for Isaac Pott's house, which was to be his headquarters.

Disease, flu, smallpox, typhus, and exposure would take one in four that winter. As life in Valley Forge became an unbearable nightmare, Washington wrote, "No history now extant can furnish an instance of an army's suffering such uncommon hardships as ours has done and bearing them with the same patience and fortitude. To see men without clothes to cover their nakedness, without blankets to lie on, without shoes (... the want of which their marches might be traced by the blood from their feet...), and submitting without a murmur, is a proof of patience and obedience which in my opinion can scarce be paralleled."[17]

As the early settlers had faced their starving times, so did the men of Valley Forge pass through their "crucible of freedom." They endured because their General endured, and made no secret of his Christian faith. Calling for divine services every Sunday, he told his men, "To the distinguished character of a Patriot, it should be our highest glory to add the more distinguished character of a Christian."[18]

"I heard a fine example today," a Lutheran pastor reported, "namely, that His Excellency General Washington rode around among his army yesterday and admonished each and every one to fear God, to put away the wickedness that has set in and become so general, and to practice the Christian virtues. From all appearances, this gentleman does not belong to the so-called world of society, for he respects God's Word, believes in the atonement through Christ, and bears himself in humility and gentleness. Therefore, the Lord God has also singularly, yea, marvelously, preserved him from harm in the midst of countless perils, ambuscades, fatigues, etc., and has hitherto graciously held him in His hand as a chosen vessel."[19]

Isaac Potts, in whose house he was quartered, was a Quaker and a pacifist. One day he came upon Washington in a secluded grove of trees in prayer. Returning home, he burst into tears. He explained to his wife, Sarah, what he had seen, and said, "If there is anyone on this earth whom the Lord will listen to, it is George Washington; and I feel a presentiment that under such a commander there can be no doubt of our eventually establishing our independence, and that God in his providence has willed it so."[20]

In February, Congress sent a committee which was shocked to find how many feet and legs froze till they became black, and it was often necessary to amputate them.

But in their weakness they were becoming stronger, more trusting in Washington and each other, more sure of the rightness of their cause. The soldiers who came through Valley Forge were tempered into an army that was committed to stay until the war was won. As it turned out, Benjamin Franklin's statement when the British captured Philadelphia, "Philadelphia took Howe," became true.

An anonymous soldier was quoted in the *Pennsylvania Packet:* "Our attention is now drawn to one point: the enemy grows weaker every day, and we are growing stronger. Our work is almost done, and with the blessing of heaven, and the valor of our worthy general, we shall soon drive these plunderers out of our country!"[21]

Like Squanto, who came just in time to meet the needs of the Pilgrims, Baron von Steuben arrived just in time to meet the pressing needs of the undisciplined Continental army.

A bemedaled German with a passion for drill and precision, a former captain in the Prussian army and staff officer of Frederick the Great, he was recommended by Benjamin Franklin who was serving as our ambassador in Paris.

Washington quickly assigned him the task of making a professional army out of the American volunteers. By April they were able to fire a crisp volley every fifteen seconds, and were marching as one. Their morale was improving along with their newfound skills.

On May 1, word reached Valley Forge that France was now an ally of the Americans. Volunteers and supplies began pouring in.

The devotion, wisdom, and caring of Washington held this army together in spite of the intrigue of ambitious officers, the failure of congress to supply his soldiers with desperately needed supplies, and the greed of the suppliers--which he despised. He watched the plot of the officers, and in due time exposed them, destroying them. At the same time his quiet strength of character won the confidence and love of his soldiers and countrymen.

While Washington was credited with holding the army together at Valley Forge, he gave the credit to God:

"It having pleased the Almighty Ruler of the universe to defend the cause of the United American States, and finally to raise up (France) a powerful friend among the princes of the earth, to establish our liberty and independence upon a lasting foundation, it becomes us to set apart a day for gratefully acknowledging the divine goodness, and celebrating the important event, which we owe to His divine interposition."[22]

In his order of May 2, 1778 at Valley Forge, he said, "It is expected that officers of all ranks will, by their attendance, set an example for their men. While we are duly performing the duty of good soldiers, we certainly ought not to be inattentive to the higher duty of religion..."[23]

Looking back over the years of strife, men saw clearly that the greatest factor in the final success of the American Colonists was the personal leadership of Washington. His lack of a mean ambition, his devotion to serving well his country and his fellow men, his unswerving faithfulness in spite of jealously or resentment, these were the traits, forged in the fires of adversity, that give him a unique and solitary place among the world's heroes.

Surrender of Cornwallis at Yorktown by John Trumbull, Capital Rotunda

CHAPTER FOUR

"...The Interposing Hand..."

"Our affairs are brought to a perilous crises, that the hand of Providence, I trust, may be more conspicuous in our deliverance," Washington wrote Major-General Armstrong, March 26, 1781. "The many remarkable interpositions of the Divine government in the hours of our deepest distress and darkness, have been too luminous to suffer me to doubt the happy issue of the present contest..."[1]

Almost a month after the surrender of Yorktown on October 19, 1781, Washington wrote Thomas McKean, President of Congress, "...I take a particular pleasure in acknowledging that the interposing Hand of Heaven, in various instances of our extensive preparation for this operation, has been most conspicuous and remarkable."[2]

First, there was the Battle of Cowpens, where the British detachment was defeated. Then Cornwallis headed for the Catawba River to cut off the retreat of the small American army and reached it just two hours after the Americans had crossed. He decided to wait until morning to cross, but during the night a storm flooded the river, delaying him further. He nearly overtook Washington on February 3, but reached the Yadkin River just after the Americans had crossed it when a sudden flood stopped him. It happened again ten days later when the Americans crossed the Dan River into friendly territory just before a storm which again put rising waters between him and Washington.

Clinton, the Commander-in-Chief of Cornwallis's army wrote, "...here the Royal Army was again stopped by a sudden rise of the water, which had only just fallen (almost miraculously) to let the enemy over, who could not else have eluded Lord Cornwallis's grasp so close was he upon their rear."

Thus, miraculously, after two years of cat and mouse maneuvering, with the Americans usually outnumbered and therefore in the role of drawing the enemy further from its bases of supply, Washington's small army escaped to chase General Cornwallis and drive him to the sea in time to see the French fleet defeat the British fleet which had been sent to help him. No one was more surprised than George Washington who knew nothing about the whereabouts of the French fleet, but was grateful he had decided to march to Yorktown when he did; and Robert Morris, who was glad he had raised the money to keep Washington's troops from going home; and Cornwallis, who was more than frustrated that he had been stopped at the York River by another of those pesky continental storms![3]

When he had attempted to evacuate his troops with the same tactic which had been used by Washington at the East River, a sudden violent storm had driven his boats down-river, and Cornwallis was forced to order the troops that had reached the far shore back and to surrender.

"Thus expired the last hope of the British Army," according to General Banistre Tarleton.[4]

Although the war would not end for another two years, both sides sensed it was over.

There was great rejoicing among the troops, but Washington remembered to order a thanksgiving service to be held the day after the surrender of Cornwallis, recommending "...that the troops not on duty should universally attend with that seriousness of deportment and gratitude of heart which the recognition of such reiterated and astonishing interposition of Providence demands of us."[5]

One of the sermons inspired by the capture of the British Army under the command of Earl Cornwallis, preached by Timothy Dwight, one of the most famous ministers of the day, was on Isaiah 59:19: "When the enemy shall come in like a flood, the spirit of the Lord shall lift up a standard against him." He pointed out that "...our most important successes, in almost every instance, have happened when we were peculiarly weak and distressed..." and concluded, "Praise the Lord, for He is good, for His mercy endureth forever."[6]

After the surrender of Cornwallis, General Washington hastened to the bedside of Martha Washington's son, John Parke Curtis, who had been his aide-de-camp at the siege of Yorktown. At his death 16 days later, weeping, he told Martha, "I adopt the two younger children as my own."[7]

He wrote the President of the Congress acknowledging the resolution of Congress and the proclamation of a day of public prayer, saying, "...The success of the combined arms against our enemies at York and Gloucester, as it affects the welfare and independence of the United States, I viewed as a most fortunate event...I take a particular pleasure in acknowledging that the enterprising hand of Heaven, in the various instances of our extensive preparations for this operation, has been most conspicuous and remarkable."[8]

In later days he said to Brigadier Nelson, "The hand of Providence has been so conspicuous in all this, that he must be worse than an infidel that lacks faith, and more than wicked, that has not gratitude enough to acknowledge his obligations."[9]

Washington saw God's hand upon the Americans even when he reported the betrayal of Matthew Arnold, who was then commander of West Point. He said, "Treason of the blackest dye was yesterday discovered...The providential train of circumstances which led to it affords the most convincing proofs that the liberties of America are the object of divine protection."[10]

The "providential train of circumstances" began when the British spy Andre, disguised in civilian clothes, mistook an American patrol for British and revealed he was a British officer. Upon searching him the Americans found secret plans for West Point and a pass signed by Arnold, but the officer in charge failed to realize the significance of what he had found. He sent Andre to Arnold to explain how he happened to have the pass signed by him and the plans. Fortunately, Major Ben Tallmadge, Washington's Chief of Intelligence, "happened" to be in the area. He had been privately concerned about Arnold for some time and, although Arnold escaped capture, West Point was saved.[11]

On October 31, 1783, George and Martha Washington and many of our leaders attended services at Princeton College Chapel celebrating and giving thanks for the signing of the Treaty of Peace between the United States and Great Britain on Sept 3 at Versailles. The official Proclamation of Peace was greeted with an indescribable outburst of rejoicing.[12]

Again and again, Washington expressed in clearest words his recognition of the divine guidance and help he had experienced. On June 8, 1783, upon disbanding his army, he issued a circular letter to the governors of all the thirteen states:

"When we consider the magnitude of the prize we contended for, the doubtful nature of the contest, and the favorable manner in which it has terminated, we shall find the greatest possible reason for gratitude and rejoicing...

"They (the citizens of America) are from this period to be considered as the actors on a most conspicuous theatre, which seems to be peculiarly designated by Providence for the display of human greatness and felicity. Here they are not only surrounded with everything, which can contribute to the completion of private and domestic enjoyment, but Heaven has crowned all its other blessing, by giving a fairer opportunity for political happiness, than any other nation has ever been favored with...The free cultivation of letters, the unbounded extension of commerce, the progressive refinement of manners, the growing liberality of sentiment, and, above all, the pure and benign light of Revelation, have had a meliorating influence on mankind and increased the blessings of society..."[13]

In his farewell address to the Armies of the United States at Rock Hill, New Jersey on November, 1783, he said, "The singular interposition of Providence in our feeble conditions were such as could scarcely escape the attention of the most observing..."[14]

In his address to Congress on December 23, 1783, he reiterated, "Happy in the confirmation of our independence and sovereignty...I resign with satisfaction the appointment I accepted with diffidence, a diffidence in my abilities to accomplish so arduous a task, which, however, was superseded by a confidence in the rectitude of our cause, the support of the supreme power of the Union, and the patronage of Heaven.

"The successful termination of the war has verified the most sanguine expectations; and my gratitude for the interposition of Providence and the assistance I have received from my countrymen, increases with every review of the momentous contest...I consider it an indispensable duty to close this last solemn act of my official life by commending the interests of our dearest country to the protection of Almighty God, and of those who have superintendence of them to His holy keeping."[15]

Washington never ceased to credit the interposing hand of God for the victorious outcome of the War of Independence. After it was over, he wrote Major-General Knox from Mt. Vernon on February 20, 1784, "I feel now, however, as I conceive a wearied traveler must do who, after treading many a painful step with a heavy burden on his shoulders, is eased of the latter, having reached the haven to which all the former were directed; and from his housetop is looking back, and tracing with an eager eye the meanders by which he escaped the quicksands and mires which lay in his way; into which none but the all-powerful Guide and Dispenser of human events could have prevented his falling."[16]

Triumph of Patriotism, Nov. 1783. National Archives

CHAPTER FIVE

The Battle For The Constitution

For the first time since its settlement by the English, America was an independent nation--and it was heady stuff. God's kingdom on earth, which had been envisioned by the Pilgrims and other early settlers, was now a reality in the opinion of many of its ministers.

John Rodgers preached a sermon on the remarkable instances of Divine Providence in the war, concluding, "...There is not an instance in history, within my recollection, of so great a revolution being effected in so short a time, and with so little loss of life and property..." He speculated on what would have happened had a lesser man assumed the generalship of the army.[1]

Timothy Wight, grandson of Jonathan Edwards and shortly to become President of Yale College, said, "God brought His little flock hither and placed it in this wilderness for the great purpose of establishing permanently the church of Christ in these vast regions of idolatry and sin, and commencing here the glorious work of salvation...here is the seed, from which this vast harvest is going to spring." Repeatedly calling for a reestablishment of the covenant relationship which our forefathers entered into with God, he said "...only if America honored the vertical and horizontal aspects of the Covenant would ...independence and happiness be fixed upon the most lasting foundations, and that Kingdom of the Redeemer...(be) highly exalted and durably established on the ruins of the Kingdom of Satan."[2]

Unfortunately, man is prone to selfishness, especially where his pocketbook is affected, and soon arguments over who would pay the war debt began to grow and become more vindictive and the United States, which had been bought at such a price, seemed destined to be divided instead of united.

Also there were deists like Thomas Jefferson for whom the God of the Bible was of secondary importance. I did a careful study of his *The Life and Morals of Jesus Christ* at the University of Virginia, which he said He had written to prove he was a disciple of Jesus, and found he had revised the Gospel of the New Testament by deleting all references to the supernatural. Affirming that Jesus was the greatest teacher who ever lived and that he read his (Jefferson's) revised version of the Bible every night, the writer of our Declaration of Independence led the "higher criticism" which gradually began to erode the *Sola Scriptura* belief that had predominated the thinking of the founding fathers. It is hard to believe his weakened deist version of a God who had left us to work out our own destiny would have enabled us to win the War of Independence!

Looking at the world from opposing basic presuppositions led to delusion and dissension after the war was won.

In every aspect of the War of Independence George Washington had led the way so that all Americans, looking back over the years of strife, saw clearly that the greatest factor in the final success of the Revolution was the personal leadership of Washington. He was the symbol of America's independence, but this hard-won independence might have been lost in the years that followed had it not been for his unselfish and brilliant leadership in the crucial years of this nation's beginning.

Although he wanted no more of public life and was content to remain at his beloved Mt. Vernon, he began to see his work was but half done--that the sacrifice and suffering of eight years would be in vain unless a strong union was formed. Unwilling to "win the war and lose the peace" as our nation has done too often, he began a letter-writing campaign to plead for the salvation of the nation, warning "...something must be done, or the fabric will fall, for it is certainly tottering."[3]

On November 5, 1786, he wrote James Madison, "We are fast emerging to anarchy and confusion. "We cannot exist long as a nation without having lodged somewhere a power which will pervade the whole Union in as energetic a manner as the authority of the State governments extend over the States."[4]

Later that year he warned John Jay, "Our Affairs are drawing rapidly to a crises," and, on May 30, 1787, he wrote Jefferson, "...the situation of the general government, if it can be called a government, is shaky indeed. Unless a remedy is soon applied, anarchy and confusion will inevitably ensue."[5]

Largely due to his efforts, Congress called a Constitutional Convention to meet in Philadelphia in May, 1787.

Unanimously elected to preside over the convention, Washington--quiet, respected, calm, fair, and patient--prevented widespread disagreements from sabotaging the meetings. The same excellent moral leadership which had succeeded during the Revolution stood him in good stead here...especially since thirty of the fifty-five delegates at the Convention had served as officers under him, and three had been his aides![6]

When some of the delegates began to show signs of moral compromise, it was Washington who said, "If, to please the people, we offer what we ourselves disapprove, how can we afterward defend our work? Let us raise a standard to which the wise and the honest can repair; the outcome is in the hands of God."[7]

Realizing the Convention needed to be largely educational, he patiently allowed them to vote 60 times on the method to be used in selecting the President. Consequently, when the more difficult problem of representation of the states came up, they were able to work out an entirely original concept in government that would protect the rights of all and prevent the larger, more powerful states from overriding the smaller ones. His patience and willingness to be reasonable resulted in their voting for our Constitution after much debate.

It had not been easy. Toward the end of June the large states were locked in an unyielding battle with the small states on the question of representation. Delegates wrote home that the attempt to forge a new government had failed and Washington wrote to Hamilton, "I almost despair of seeing a favorable issue to the proceedings of our convention."[8]

On June 18, 1787, when it looked as though the Constitution would be stillborn, and many threatened to leave, Benjamin

Franklin, the oldest signer of The Declaration of Independence and the oldest member of the Constitutional Convention, reminded the delegates there had been daily prayers in that place during the Revolution and that they had been "graciously answered." He then moved that their meetings begin with prayer.[9] (Deists believe God has left us to work out our affairs on our own, without His help, so these were hardly the words of a deist!)

Why George Washington had neglected starting their meetings with prayer we are not told. Perhaps it was in order for Benjamin Franklin to go on record regarding his belief in God's intervening hand in this nation's destiny. Perhaps God wanted to show us what the founding fathers learned during "The Great Awakening"-- that man, without God, can do no good thing, and that with God all things are possible!

We do know that every principle Washington considered necessary was incorporated in the constitution within weeks after Franklin's motion was passed.

On July 20, 1787, Washington wrote his friend, Jonathan Trumbull, "...we may, with a kind of pious and grateful exaltation, trace the finger of Providence through those dark and mysterious events, which first induced the States to appoint a general convention, and then led them one after another by such steps as were best calculated to effect the object into an adoption of the system recommended by that general convention; thereby laying a lasting foundation for tranquility and happiness, when we had but too much reason to fear that confusion and misery were coming rapidly upon us. That the same good Providence may still continue to protect and prevent us from dashing the cup of national felicity, just as it has been lifted to our lips, is the earnest prayer of, my dear sir, your faithful friend."[10]

On September 18, 1787, Washington affixed his distinctive signature to the Constitution of the United States, followed by all but three members present. He then went to his lodgings "...to meditate upon the momentous work which had been executed."

The next day, he wrote Lafayette, "It is the result of four months deliberation. It is now a child of fortune, to be fostered by some and buffeted by others." But history has affirmed that it has stood the test of time better than any other similar document in the history of the world and has been lauded by men of many nations. William E. Gladstone, Prime Minister of England, echoed all the others when he characterized our Constitution as "...the greatest work of its kind ever turned out by the mind and purpose of man."[11]

Washington used his influence to secure the adoption of the Constitution by writing letters, and, when it was finally ratified by all the states, James Monroe wrote to Jefferson, who was still in Paris, "Be assured General Washington's influence carried this government."[12]

Always conscientious and careful in following through, Washington wrote to leaders in the various states, urging that friends of the Constitution be elected to Congress in order to make it work.

The whole country turned to him as their choice for President but, weary and in poor health, he held back until Alexander Hamilton said to him, "In a matter so essential to the well-being of society as the prosperity of a newly instituted government, a citizen of so much consequence as yourself to its success has no option but to lend his service."[13]

He went to the office of the President, as he wrote on April 1, 1789, with "...feelings not unlike those of a culprit who is going to the place of execution...Integrity and firmness is all I can promise."[14]

He was to draw on these many times in the difficult days of his presidency as he strove to institute a government true to the Constitution.

At a great civic banquet in Philadelphia, he replied to a congratulatory address on his election by saying, "When I contemplate the interposition of Providence, as it was manifested in guiding us through the Revolution, in preparing us for the reception of a general government, and in conciliating the good will of the people of America towards one another after its adoption, I feel myself oppressed and almost overwhelmed with a sense of the divine munificence. I feel that nothing is due to my personal agency in all these complicated and wonderful events, except what can simply be attributed to the exertions of an honest zeal for the good of my country.

"I have distressing apprehensions that I shall not be able to justify the too exalted expectations of my countrymen. I am supported under the pressure of such uneasy reflections by a confidence that the most gracious being, who has hitherto watched over the interests and averted the perils of the United States, will never suffer so fair an inheritance to become a prey to anarchy, despotism, or any other species of oppression."[15]

Shortly before leaving for New York to take the oath of office, he visited his 82-year-old mother, who was ill with cancer.

"You will see me no more," she said. "My great age, and the disease which is fast approaching my vitals, warn me that I shall not be long in this world. I trust in God that I may be somewhat prepared for a better. But go, George, fulfill the high destinies which Heaven appears to have intended you for; go, my son, and may that Heaven's and a mother's blessing be with you always."

Sadly he wept and embraced her. It was indeed the last time he was to see his mother on this earth.[16]

His journey from Mt. Vernon began with a public dinner in Alexandria with neighbors and friends. Deeply moved by words of affection by the mayor, he replied, "All that remains for me is to commit myself and you to the care of that beneficent Being who, on a former occasion, happily brought us together after a long and distressing separation. Perhaps the same gracious Providence will again indulge me. But words fail me. Unutterable sentiments must be left to more expressive silence, while from an aching heart, I bid you my affectionate friends and neighbors, farewell."[17]

As he travelled along roads lined with soldiers and citizens, there was the continual ringing of bells and firing of guns. At Baltimore, a cavalcade of citizens escorted him amid a roaring welcome.

At Philadelphia he mounted a horse in the midst of a troop of calvary and rode into the city beneath triumphal arches for a day of public celebration.

At Trenton there was an arch of triumph and adoring young ladies walked before him strewing flowers in his path and singing songs of praise and gratitude.

At Elizabethtown Point the committees of Congress met him and he was rowed to the city of New York by thirteen pilots in white uniform, accompanied by music and song from a long procession of barges while ships in the harbour, covered with flags, fired salutes in his honor.

From Mt. Vernon to New York, it had been one long triumphal march--a simple outpouring of gratitude and reverence from the hearts of the people for a great man they loved and trusted.[18]

The leadership of George Washington was responsible for a change of Government from nearly 4000 years of empires, kingdoms, and hereditary rulers, to government by the consent of the governed. In the years to come many other countries were to try to build on this model, so that the Pilgrims vision of being "...but steppingstones..." became literally true. When they failed it was because they didn't understand that it was only possible through following the biblical principles of those Pilgrims.

Twice the Congressional Congress had given Washington the power of a dictator and twice he was offered the position of King, but he remained true to the belief that power should and must remain in the hands of the people. He spent the rest of his life insuring that it would, for which we and the rest of the world should be grateful.

With the same wisdom and restraint he had used in winning the War of Independence, he quietly and steadily guided it through to the high standard he had proclaimed at his election, repudiating the cheap political compromises of those who sought to please the people at the expense of the national interest.

He had labored long and hard to see that the Constitution was ratified and, after the ratification, he had written Benjamin Lincoln (on June 29, l788):

"...No country upon Earth ever had it more in its power to attain these blessings (happy at home and respectable abroad) than United America. Wondrously strange then, and much to be regretted indeed would it be were we to neglect the means and depart from the road which Providence has pointed us to so plainly; I cannot believe it will ever come to pass. The Great Governor of the Universe has led us too long and too far on the road to happiness and glory, to forsake us in the midst of it. By folly and improper conduct, proceeding from a variety of causes, we may now and then get bewildered; but I hope ánd trust that there is good sense and virtue enough left to recover the right path before we shall be entirely lost."

Of the Constitution he wrote, "The structure has been erected by architects of consummate skill and fidelity; its foundations are solid; its compartments are beautiful as well as useful; its arrangements are full of wisdom and order and its defenses are impregnable from without. It has been reared for immortality, if the work of man may greatly aspire to such a title."

But he hastened to warn, "It may, nevertheless, perish in an hour by the folly, or corruption, or negligence of its only keepers, THE PEOPLE. Republics are created by the virtue, public spirit, and intelligence of the citizens. They fall when the wise are banished from the public councils, because they dare to be honest, and the profligates are rewarded because they flatter the people in order to betray them."[19]

"...only keepers, THE PEOPLE," please take note!

The Day's Beginning, 1786, J.L.G. Ferris, Archives of 76, Bay Village, Ohio.

CHAPTER SIX

President Washington Warns Our Nation

On the first Inauguration Day, April 30, 1789, religious services were held in the churches of America and God's blessing invoked in behalf of the new government.

At twelve noon, President-elect Washington moved in procession to Federal Hall in Wall Street and proceeded to the Balcony below which an enormous crowd of people hailed him with loud applause.

Chancellor Livingston of New York administered the oath of office, whereupon Washington laid his hand on a large open Bible held by Secretary of State Otis and answered solemnly, "I swear-- so help me God!" He then bowed reverently and kissed the Bible.

As crowds below sent up a shout of joy and church bells rang out amid the roar of artillery, he returned to the Senate chamber to deliver his Inaugural Address:

"Such being the impressions under which I have, in obedience to the public summons, repaired to the present station, it would be peculiarly improper to omit, in this first official act, my fervent supplications to that Almighty Being who rules over the universe, who presides in the councils of nations, and whose providential aid can supply every human defect, that His benediction may consecrate to the liberties and happiness of the people of the United States a government instituted by themselves for these essential purposes and may enable every instrument employed in its administration to execute with success the functions allotted to his charge.

"In tendering this homage to the great Author of every public and private good, I assure myself that it expresses your sentiments not less than my own, nor those of my fellow Citizens at large, less than either...No people can be bound to acknowledge and adore the invisible Hand which conducts the affairs of men more than those of the United States. Every step by which they have advanced to the character of an independent nation seems to have been distinguished by some token of providential agency.

"These reflections, arising out of the present crisis, have forced themselves too strongly on my mind to be suppressed. You will join with me, I trust, in thinking that there are none under the influence of which the proceedings of a new and free government can more auspiciously commence. We ought to be no less persuaded that the propitious smiles of Heaven can never be expected on a nation that disregards the eternal rules of order and right, which Heaven itself has ordained.

"Having thus imparted to you my sentiments, as they have been awakened by the occasion which brings us together, I shall take my present leave; but not without resorting once more to the benign parent of the human race, in humble supplication that, since He has been pleased to favor the American people with opportunities for deliberating in perfect tranquillity, and dispositions for deciding with unparalleled unanimity on a form of government for the security of their union and the advancement of their happiness, so His divine blessing may be equally conspicuous in the enlarged views, the temperate consultations, and the wise measures on which the success of this government may depend."[1]

Fully aware he would be walking "on untrodden ground," and that anything he might do could set a precedent, his acts were carefully and deliberately aimed to form a strong and righteous government based on the laws of God and the Constitution.

Soon after his inauguration, he was stricken with a violent illness which lasted for six weeks. He asked his physician to tell him the probable result, saying, "Do not flatter me with vain hopes. I am not afraid to die, and therefore can bear the worst."

When the doctor acknowledged his concerns, Washington replied, "Whether tonight or twenty years hence, makes no difference. I know that I am in the hands of a good Providence."[2]

The following October 3, 1789, fully recovered, he issued the first National Thanksgiving proclamation.[3]

The same year Washington became president, the French Revolution began. Jefferson, as Secretary of State, was determined the United States should join France, ignoring the violent excesses and bloody massacres of the revolutionists and the fact that he had been appointed to represent the President. He had been greatly influenced during his stay in France by the humanistic philosophies of the French revolutionaries, seeing Jesus as the greatest teacher who ever lived, but denying his deity. He acknowledged God but saw Him as the One who had created everything but had left the world to work out its own problems with no interference from Him.

Because of the support of the French for our revolution, it was popular to support France, but Washington refused to be stampeded by Jefferson and his followers and saved the new government from destroying itself by becoming a satellite of France in a revolution totally different from our own.[4]

Washington faced many other severe tests as President, including the Whiskey Rebellion, Indian warfare on our western borders which was incited by the British, and the Jay Treaty with Britain, but his firmness finally caused him to come through with the approval of the people.

Jefferson complained, "Such is the popularity of the President that the people will support him in whatever he will do or will not do, without appealing to their own reason, or to anything but their feelings toward him."[5]

A better opinion of our first President was given by John Marshall (who fought in the Revolution and served as Chief Justice of the Supreme Court for 24 years from 1801-1825) to whom the *International Encyclopedia* attributed the greatest contribution to American jurisprudence made by any judge. He said: "Endowed by nature with sound judgment and an accurate and discriminating mind...he was guided by an unvarying sense of moral right, which would tolerate only those means which would bear the most rigid examination; by fairness of intention which neither sought or required disguise; and by a purity of virtue which was untainted."[6]

It is significant that the American people whom Washington trusted chose such a dedicated Christian to lead them and further proof that this was a Christian-oriented nation from the beginning.

Among the accomplishments of the new government was the assumption of war-time debts by the Federal Government, a National Bank law, a law for the assessment and collection of taxes, various parts of government set up including the State Department, War Department, Attorney General's office, and Post Office Department. In addition they secured peace on the western borders and gave us the *Bill of Rights*.

Unanimously elected twice without opposition, Washington was urged to run for a third term but he refused. Foreign relations were much improved, the country was prospering as never before, and he was tired.

He did issue a warning to the nation months before leaving office. It came to be considered next in importance to *The Constitution* and *The Declaration of Independence* and is called *Washington's Farewell Address.*[7]

After stating the reasons for his retirement, he said:

"Here perhaps I ought to stop. But a solicitude for your welfare which cannot end with my life, and the apprehension of danger natural to that solicitude, urge me on an occasion like the present to offer to your solemn contemplation and to recommend to your frequent review some sentiments which are the result of much reflection, of no inconsiderable observation, and which appear to me all-important to the permanency of your felicity as a people..."

"Interwoven as is the love of liberty with every ligament of your hearts, no recommendation of mine is necessary to fortify or confirm the attachment.

"The unity of government which constitutes you one people is also now dear to you. It is justly so, for it is a main pillar in the edifice of your real independence, the support of your tranquility at home, your peace abroad, of your safety, of your prosperity, of that very liberty which you so highly prize. But it is easy to foresee that from different causes and from different quarters much pains will be taken, many artifices employed, to weaken in your minds the conviction of this truth, as this is the point in our political fortress against which the batteries of internal and external enemies will be most constantly and actively (though often covertly and insidiously) directed. It is of infinite moment that you should properly estimate the immense value of your national union to your collective and individual happiness; that you should cherish a cordial, habitual, and immovable attachment to it; accustoming yourselves to think and speak of it as of the palladium of your political safety and prosperity; watching for its preservation with jealous anxiety; discountenancing whatever may suggest even a suspicion that it can in any event be abandoned, and indignantly frowning upon the first dawning of any attempt to alienate any portion of our country from the rest or to enfeeble the sacred ties which now link together the various parts...

"These considerations speak a persuasive language to every reflecting and virtuous mind, and exhibit the continuance of the UNION as a primary object of Patriotic desire...There will always be reason to distrust the patriotism of those who in any quarter may endeavor to weaken its bands...

"This Government, the offspring of your own choice, uninfluenced and unawed, adopted upon full investigation and mature deliberation, completely free in its principles, in the distribution of its powers, uniting security with energy, and containing within itself a provision for its own amendment, has a just claim to your confidence and your support. Respect for its authority, compliance with its laws, acquiescence in its measures, are duties enjoined by the fundamental maxims of true liberty. The basis of our political system is the right of the people to make and to alter their constitutions of government. But the constitution which at any time exists, till changed by an explicit and authentic act of the whole people, is sacredly obligatory upon all. The very idea of the power and the right of the people to establish government presupposes the duty of every individual to obey the established government...

"I have already intimated to you the danger of parties in the State with particular reference to the founding of them on geographical discriminations. Let me now take a more comprehensive view and warn you in the most solemn manner against the baneful effects of the spirit of party generally...

"It is important, likewise, that the habits of thinking in a free country should inspire caution in those entrusted with its administration to confine themselves within their respective constitutional sphere, avoiding in the exercise of the powers of one department to encroach upon another. The spirit of encroachment tends to consolidate the powers of all departments in one, and thus to create, whatever the form of government, a real despotism.

Of all the dispositions and habits which lead to political prosperity, religion and morality are indispensable supports....And let us with caution indulge the supposition that morality can be maintained without religion. Whatever may be conceded to the influence of refined education on minds of peculiar structure, reason and experience both forbid us to expect that national morality can prevail in exclusion of religious principle...

"It is substantially true that virtue or morality is the necessary spring of popular government. The rule indeed extends with more or less force to every species of free government. Who that is a sincere friend to it can look with indifference upon attempts to shake the foundation of the fabric? Promote, then, as an object of primary importance, institutions for the general diffusion of knowledge. In proportion as the structure of a government gives force to public opinion, it is essential that public opinion should be enlightened...

"Observe good faith and justice toward all nations. Cultivate peace and harmony with all...

"In the execution of such a plan nothing is more essential than that permanent, inveterate antipathies against particular nations and passionate attachments for others should be excluded, and that in place of them just and amicable feelings toward all should be cultivated...

"Against the insidious wiles of foreign influence (I conjure you to believe me, fellow citizens) the jealousy of a free people ought to be constantly awake, since history and experience prove that foreign influence is one of the most baneful foes of republican government...

"It is our true policy to steer clear of permanent alliances with any portion of the foreign world, so far, I mean, as we are now at liberty to do it; for let me not be understood as capable of patronizing infidelity to existing engagements. I hold the maxim no less applicable to public than to private affairs that honesty is always the best policy. I repeat, therefore, let those engagements be observed in their genuine sense. But in my opinion it is unnecessary and would be unwise to extend them...

"Though in reviewing the incidents of my Administration I am unconscious of intentional error, I am nevertheless too sensible of my defects not to think it probable that I may have committed many errors. Whatever they may be, I fervently beseech the Almighty to avert or mitigate the evils to which they may tend...

"...actuated by that fervent love toward it which is so natural to a man who views it as the native soil of himself and his progenitors for several generations, I anticipate with pleasing expectation that retreat in which I promise myself to realize without alloy the sweet enjoyment of partaking in the midst of my fellow citizens the benign influence of good laws under a free government--the ever favorite object of my heart, and the happy reward, as I trust, of our mutual cares, labors, and dangers."[7]

Now sixty-four years of age, having paid a tremendous price for his physical and emotional service to his country, Washington returned to his beloved Martha and to Mt. Vernon, which had also taken a tremendous beating through neglect during his long absence. He at once set to work to restore his beautiful home and soon the hospitality for which it had been famous before the war was drawing people from all over the nation and other countries.

Three years later he returned from work on the farm, chilled from the snow and very ill. Always responsible, he chose from two wills, had one destroyed and gave the other to Martha. Soon the agony of trying to breath became too much. Uttering the words, "'Tis well," and "Father of mercies, take me to thyself," he breathed his last breath.[8]

The funeral oration was delivered on Thursday, December 26, 1799 by Major-General Henry Lee, member of Congress from Virginia. Lee had served under him during the war, and afterward in the civil department, and was chosen for the honor by Congress.

It was in this oration Washington was called, "First in war, first in peace, and first in the hearts of his countrymen."

Lee added, "He was second to none in the humble and endearing scenes of private life...his example was edifying to all around him as were the effects of that example lasting."[9]

It was said of him that such was his character, "...that even in England not one reflection was ever cast, or the least disrespectful word uttered against him."[10]

According to the tradition of the New York Indians, "Alone, of all white men, he has been admitted to the Indian Heaven, because of his justice to the Red men. He lives in a great palace, built like a fort. All the Indians, as they go to Heaven, pass by, and he himself is in his uniform, a sword at his side, walking to and fro. They bow reverently, with great humility. He returns the salute, but says nothing."[11]

"He was the most supremely silent of the great men of action that the world can show," wrote Henry Cabot Lodge. "...who is not given to words for their own sake, and who never talks about himself...He had abundant power of words and could use them with much force and point when he was so minded, but he never used them needlessly or to hide his meaning, and he never talked about himself. He did as great work as has fallen to the lot of men, he wrote volumes of correspondence, he talked with innumerable men and women, and of himself he said nothing."[12]

And so ended the earthly life of "...the noblest figure that ever stood in the forefront of a nation's life."[13]

At his death on December 14, 1799, Congress passed a resolution declaring February 22 as a day of remembrance. Adams continued the observance of that day, but Jefferson held no observances. Recognition of his birthday became occasional and politically partisan until 1832, the centenary of Washington's Birthday, when the observance was widened. On the 200th anniversary the period of festivities lasted from February 22 to Thanksgiving. Squares were renamed for him; at least 121 post offices and one state and counties in 32 states bear his name. The highest building in our nation's capital is the Washington Monument. It stands in the center of Washington D.C. and has been likened to "The sword

149

of the Spirit," the only offensive weapon in the Bible list of the armour of God, Ephesians 6:17. "And take the helmet of salvation (which someone has likened to the dome of the Capitol Building) and the sword of the Spirit, which is the word of God."

That's where America began! This was the solid rock foundation on which she has built. May we always trust in God and His Word and may God always bless America!

Scene from the Signing of the Constitution, by Christy, S. wing of Capitol

REFERENCES CELEBRATIONS OF A NATION--
Early American Holidays

THANKSGIVING--THE FIRST AMERICAN HOLIDAY

Chapter 1--Who Were These Pilgrims?
1. *History of the Pilgrims,* by Daniel Neal, 1731
2. *The Evolution of the English Bible,* by H. W. Hoare, 1901
3. *Christian History of the Constitution of the United States of America,* by Verna M. Hall, 1966, p. 31
4. *Ibid,* p. 31
5. *"* p. 31
6. *The Geneva Bible,* Introduction to the Facsimile Edition, 1969, p. 20; *The Scottish Reformation,* by Gordon Donaldson
7. *History of Plimouth Plantation,* by William Bradford, Excerpts from the original manuscript written 1647, Christian History of the Constitution of the United States of America, by Verna M. Hall, 1966, p. 193

Chapter 2--Why Did They Come To Plymouth Rock?
1. *The Geneva Bible,* Matthew 28:18-20
2. *First Charter For Colonizing Virginia, April 10/20, 1606*
3. *The Holy Bible,* Nehemiah 9:7-8
4. *The Works of John Robinson,* by Robert Ashton, 1851
5. *Of Plimouth Plantation,* by William Bradford, p. 72
6. *Ibid,* p. 76
7. *The Christian History of the Constitution of the United States,* by Verna M. Hall, 1975, p. 184
8. *Of Plimouth Plantation* by William Bradford, p. 85-89
9. *The Puritans,* by Perry Miller & Thomas H. Johnson, Vol. I, p. 246
10. *Of Plimouth Plantation,* by William Bradford, p. 89.
11. *The American Covenant--The Untold Story,* by Foster/Swanson, Ltd. Ed., 1981, p. 84
12. *The Holy Bible,* Matthew 13:24-30
13. *The Light and the Glory,* by Peter Marshall and David Manuel, Fleming H. Revell, 1977, p. 117
14. *Ibid,* p. 118-119
15. *Of Plimouth Plantation,* by William Bradford, p. 85-96

Chapter 3--Why Was The Mayflower Compact So Important?
1. *The American Covenant--The Untold Story,* by Foster/Swanson, 1981 Ltd. Ed., p. iv

2. *The Holy Bible,* I Samuel 8:6-22
3. *The Christian History of the American Revolution,* by Verna M. Hall, xxvi'
4. *The Holy Bible,* James 1:25
5. *Of Plimouth Plantation,* by William Bradford, p. 103
6. *Christian History of the Constitution of the United States of America,* by Verna M. Hall, p. 204-205
7. *The Holy Bible,* Numbers 13:27
8. *Of Plimouth Plantation,* by William Bradford, p. 103
9. *The Holy Bible,* Genesis 12:3b
10. *Ibid,* II Chronicles 7:14

Chapter 4--Why Did These Christians Suffer So?

1. *Of Plimouth Plantation,* by William Bradford, Wright & Potter Edition, p. 13
2. Christian History of the Constitution of the United States of America, by Verna M. Hall, p.205-206
3. *Ibid.* p. 237-238
4. " p. 239-240

Chapter 5--Why Were They So Thankful?

1. *They Knew They Were Pilgrims,* edited by L. D. Geller, p. 25-31; *The Light and the Glory,* by Peter Marshall and David Manuel, 1977, p. 130
2. *The Holy Bible,* Genesis 50:20
3. *They Knew They Were Pilgrims,* edited by L. D. Geller, p. 25-31
4. *Ibid*
5. *The Holy Bible,* Luke 6:38
6. *Christian History of the Constitution of the United States of America,* by Verna M. Hall, p. 208
7. *Ibid,* p. 208
8. " p. 209
9. " p. 210
10. " p. 211
11. " p. 212
12. " p. 213-214
13. *The Holy Bible;* I Timothy 5:8
14. *Christian History of the Constitution of the United States of America,* by Verna M. Hall, p. 214
15. *Ibid,* p. 215
16. " p. 217

Chapter 6--What Have These Pilgrims To Do With Us?
1. *Teaching and Learning America's Christian History*, by Rosalie J. Slater, 1965, p. 178
2. *Christian History Of the Constitution of the United States of America*, by Verna M. Hall, p. 182, Excerpt from *The Pilgrim Republic*, by John Goodwin, 1888
3. *The Great Seal of the United States*, U.S. State Department
4. *Of Plimouth Plantation*, by William Bradford
5. *The Canterbury Tales*, by Geoffrey Chaucer
6. *Christian History of the Constitution of the United States of America*, by Verna M. Hall, p. 183, From Preface to *History of the Puritans, 1731*, by John Overton Choales, 1844 Reprint
7. *Teaching and Learning America's Christian History*, by Rosalie J. Slater, p. 178
8. *The Writings of George Washington*, Compiled by Jared Sparks, 1834-7.Vol.XII, p. 119
9. *Celebrations*, by Robert J. Myers, 1972, p. 279

THE FOURTH OF JULY--BIRTH OF A NATION

Chapter 1--At Long Last, The Birth of a Christian Nation
1. *Adams Family Correspondence*, compiled by L. H. Butterfield
2. *This Nation Under God*, by Charles E. Kistler, p. 73
3. "The Gettysburg Address," by Abraham Lincoln, Lincoln Memorial, *Encyclopedia Americana*
4. *Signers of the Declaration of Independence, Founders of a Nation*, by David C. Whitney, 1964, p.10
5. *The Holy Bible*, John 8:36
6. *Ibid*, Matthew 28:18

Chapter 2--Where Were These Revolutionaries Coming From?
1. *Our Presbyterian Heritage*, by Paul Carlson, 1973, p.18
2. *Ibid*, p. 19
3. " p. 18
4. " p. 19
5. " p. 20
6. " p. 19
7. " p. 19
8. " p. 23-24
9. " p. 25

10. " p. 24
11. " p. 50
12. " p. 25
13. " p. 27-28
14. *The Holy Bible,* Romans 8:28-29
15. *Our Presbyterian Heritage,* p. 38
16. *Ibid,* p. 39
17. " p. 39
18. " p. 40
19. " p. 41; *The Holy Bible,* Psalm 119:130; Job 8:36
20. " p. 45
21. *Our Presbyterian Heritage,* by Paul Carlson, 1973, p. 55
22. " p. 55
23. " p. 56-59
24. " p. 63
25. *Eerdmans' Handbook to Christianity in America,* 1983, p. 96-97
26. *Our Presbyterian Heritage,* by Paul Carlson, 1973, p.13
27. *Ibid,* p. 14

Chapter 3--What Was The Revolution All About?

1. *Eerdmans' Handbook to Christianity in America,* 1983, p. 130
2. *Ibid,* p. 102
3. " p. 103-105
4. " p. 106-112
5. " p. 114
6. " p. 113-114
7. " p. 116
8. *The American Covenant--The Untold Story,* by Marshall Foster and Mary-Elaine Swanson, 1981, p. 4-5
9. *Eerdmans' Handbook To Christianity in America,* p.137
10. *The Holy Bible,* Galatians 5:1
11. *Signers of the Declaration of Independence, Founders of Freedom,* by David C. .Whitney, 1964, p. 34-35
12. *The Light and the Glory,* by Marshall/Foster, 1977, p. 265
13. *Signers of the Declaration of Independence, Founders of Liberty,* by David C. Whitney, p. 48
14. *Pictorial History of the American Revolution,* by Rupert Furneaux, 1973, p. 26
15. *Milestones of American Liberty,* by Milton Meltzer, 1961, p.17

Chapter 4--Who Were These Revolutionaries?

1. *The Colonial Spirit,* by David C. Whitney, 1974. p. 5
2. *Signers of the Declaration of Independence, Founders of Freedom,* 1964, p. 26-29
3. *Ibid,* p. 98-103
4. " p. 86
5. *The American Covenant--The Untold Story,* by Marshall Foster and Mary-Elaine Swanson, 1981, p. ll
6. *Benjamin Franklin,* by Carl Van Doren, 1938, p. 7
7. *Ibid,* p. l2-33
8. *Signers of the Declaration of Independence, Founders of Freedom,* by David C. Whitney,1964, p. 89
9. *Benjamin Franklin,* by Carl Van Doren, l938, p. 777-779
10. *Signers of the Declaration of Independence, Founders of Freedom,* by David C. Whitney, 1964, p.230-232
11. *Ibid,* p. 46-51
12. " p. 33-44
13. " p. 58-62
14. " p. 61-62
15. " p. 26-29
16. *Milestones to American Liberty,* by Milton Meltzer, 1834, insert at beginning of book.

Chapter 5--Two Proclamations--What Price Liberty?

1. *Christian History of the American Revolution,* by Verna M. Hall, p. 506 (insert)
2. *Christian History of the American Revolution,* by Verna M. Hall, p. 506 (insert)
3. *History of the United States,* by George Bancroft, l838, (Third Edition) Vol. II p. 99
4. *Ibid,* p. 229
5. *Christian History of the American Revolution,* by Verna M. Hall, p. 506 (insert); The Wall, sermon reprinted by Samuel Langdon, p. 364-373
6. *This Nation Under God,* by Charles E. Kistler, l924, p. 56
7. *The Rights of the Colonists,* by Samuel Adams, 1772
8. *Signers of the Declaration of Independence, Founders of Freedom,* by David C. Whitney, l964, p. 49
9. *Ibid,* p. 145
10. " p. 145-146

11. " p. 143
12. " p. 144
13. " p. 144

Chapter 6--"...Proclaim Liberty Throughout the Land...
  1. *Signers of the Declaration of Independence, Founders of Freedom,* by David C. Whitney, 1964, p. 44
  2. *Ibid,* p. 44
  3. *George Washington The Christian,* by William J. Johnson, 1919, p. 63-66; *The Life Of George Washington* by "Washington Irving, Vol.I, 1894, p.461
  4. *Signers of the Declaration of Independence, Founders of Freedom,* by David C. Whitney, 1964, p. 20
  5. *Ibid,* p. 38
  6. *Pictorial History of the American Revolution,* by Rupert Furneaux, p. 104 insert
  7. *Signers of the Declaration of Independence, Founders of Freedom,* by David C. Whitney, p. 190-191
  8. *This Nation Under God,* by Chas. E. Kistler, 1924, p.71
  9. *Signers of the Declaration of Independence, Founders of Freedom,* by David C.Whitney, p. 38.
 10. *Milestones to American Liberty,* by Milton Meltzer, 1961, p. 27-29

GEORGE WASHINGTON'S BIRTHDAY--
THE FATHER OF OUR NATION
Chapter 1--The Education of George Washington
  1. *In the American Grain,* by William Carlos Williams, p.149
  2. *Washington, The Indispensable Man,* By James T. Flexner
  3. *Appleton's Cyclopedia of American Biography,* Vol.VI, p. 383
  4. *The Life of General Washington,* by Mason L. Weems, p.62
  5. *The Making of George Washington,* by William H. Wilbur, p. 253
  6. *Ibid,* p. 253-254
  7. *George Washington the Christian,* by John Stockton Littell, 1913, p. 5
  8. *George Washington The Christian,* by William J. Johnston, 1976, p. 16-17
  9. *Life of George Washington,* by Washington Irving, 1815, Vol. 1, p. 49

10. *The Making of George Washington,* by Gen. William H. Wilbur, 1970, p. 56
11. *George Washington's Rules of Conduct,* by Montcure D. Conway, 1890, p. 178-180
12. *George Washington the Christian,* by John Stockton Littell, 1913, p. 70.
13. *Washington's Barbados Journal,* by J. M. Toner, 1751-2
14. *George Washington The Christian,* by William J. Johnston, 1919, p. 23-24
15. *Washington's Prayers,* by W. Hergot Burt, 1907
16. *Life of General Washington,* by John N. Norton, 1870, p. 34
17. *The Writings of George Washington,* by Jared Sparks, 1834-7, Vol. II, p. 43
18. *The Story of Mary Washington,* by Marion Harland, 1892, p. 91
19. *The Writings of George Washington,* by Jared Sparks, 1834-7, Vol. II, p. 89
20. *Ibid,* p.41-42; *Recollections and Private Memoirs of Washington,* by George Washington Park Curtis, 1828
21. *The Making of George Washington,* by Gen. William H. Wilbur, 1970, p. 29-30
22. *The Man of Mind,* Vol. 1, by Professor Albert Bushnell Hart, G.W. Bicentennial Edition, p. 17

Chapter 2 -- "With a Firm Reliance On the Providence of God..."
1. *The Making of George Washington,* by William H. Wilbur, p. 182
2. Appleton's *Cyclopedia of American Biography,* Vol. VI p. 383; *George Washington The Christian,* by William J. Johnston, 1919 p. 67
3. *A Fairfax Friendship, The Complete Correspondence Between George Washington and Bryan Fairfax.* Edited by Donald M. Sweig and Elizabeth S. Davids 1982, p. 63-64
4. *The Life of General Washington,* by Mason L. Weems, 1808, p. 182
5. *The Life of George Washington,* by John N. Norton, 1870, p. 145
6. The Writings of George Washington, by Jared Sparks, 1834-7, Vol. III, p. 49
7. *Ibid,* p. 240

8. The Cambridge of 1776, with the diary of Dorothy Dudley, p. 59
9. *The Light and the Glory,* by Peter Marshall and David Manuel, 1977, p. 297-298
10. "Washington's First Victory", Boston *Globe,* March 7,1976, p. 34
11. "Providence Rides a Storm,", by James Thomas Flexner, American Heritage series, Vol. XIX, No. 1, p. 17
12. George Washington The Christian, by William J. Johnson, p. 78
13. *Ibid,* p. 79
14. *The Writings of George Washington,* Vol. III, by Jared Sparks, p. 341
15. Ibid, Vol. IX, p. 337; *George Washington The Christian,* by William J. Johnson, p. 77-78

Chapter 3--Forged In The Valleys
1. The Writings of George Washington, by Jared Sparks, 1834-1837, Vol. III, p. 449
2. *Ibid,* p. 404
3. *Rebels and Redcoats,* by Scheer and Rankin, p. 167
4. *The Light and the Glory,* by Peter Marshall and David Manuel, 1977, p. 315
5. *The Spirit of 1776,* by Commager and Morris, 1958, p. 464
6. *George Washington,* by Henry Cabot Lodge, 1889 & 1898, Vol. I, p. 178-179
7. *The Spirit of 1776,* by Commager and Morris, 1958, p. 230-233
8. *Ibid,* p. 241
9. " p. 265-266
10. " p. 265-266
11. " p. 265
12. *George Washington,* by Henry Cabot Lodge, 1889, p. 179-183
13. *The Spirit of 1776,* by Commager and Morris, 1958, p. 513-519
14. *The Light and the Glory,* by Peter Marshall and David Manuel, 1977, p. 318
15. *Ibid,* p. 319
16. " p. 324
17. *George Washington,* by Douglas Southall Freeman, Vol. 4, p. 621

18. *Revolutionary Orders of General Washington,* selected from MSS of John Whiting, Edited by Henry Whiting, 1844
19. *Notebook of Colonial Clergyman,* by Henry Melchoir Muhlenberg, p. 195
20. *The Life of George Washington,* by Mason L. Weems, 1808, p. 104
21. *Ordeal at Valley Forge,* by J. J. Stoudt, 1963, p. 146
22. *This Nation Under God,* by Charles E. Kistler, 1924, p. 74-75
23. *The Pictorial Field-Book of the Revolution,* by Benson J. Lossing, 1886, Vol. II, p. 140

Chapter 4--"....The Interposing Hand..."
1. *The Writings of George Washington,* by Jared Sparks, 1834-7, Vol. VII, p. 462
2. *George Washington The Christian,* by William J.Johnson, 1976, p. 133
3. *The Light and the Glory,* by Marshall and Manuel, p. 330
4. *A New Age Begins,* by Page Smith, 1976, p. 1704
5. *Orderly Book of the Siege of Yorktown,* Edited by Horace W. Smith, 1865, p. 47
6. *The Light and the Glory,* by Peter Marshall and David Manuel, 1977, p. 332-333
7. *Recollections of Private Memoirs of George Washington,* by George Washington Park Curtis, 1860, p. 38
8. *The Writings of George Washington,* by Jared Sparks, 1834-7, Vol. VIII, p. 207
9. *George Washington and Religion,* by Paul F. Boller, Jr. 1963, p. 106
10. *Voices of 1776,* by Richard Wheeler, 1972, p. 382
11. *Ibid,* p. 134
12. *George Washington The Christian,* by William J. Johnson, 1976, p. 143
13. *The Writings of George Washington,* by Jared Sparks, 1834-7, Vol. VIII, p. 440, 444, 452.
14. *Ibid,* p. 492, 496
15. " p. 504-505
16. " Vol. IX, p. 22

Chapter 5--Washington's Battle For the Constitution
1. *The Light and the Glory*, by Marshall and Manuel, p. 337-338
2. *Ibid*, p. 338-339
3. *Calvinism Vs Democracy*, by Stephen E. Berk, p. 24
4. *The Making of George Washington*, by William H. Wilbur, p.209
5. *Ibid*, p. 209
6. " p. 216
7. *The Critical Period of American History*, by John Fisk, p. 274-275
8. *The Making of George Washington*, by William H. Wilbur, p. 213
9. *The American Covenant--The Untold Story*, by Marshall Foster and Mary-Elaine Swanson, 1981 p. 11
10. *The Writings of George Washington*, Vol. IX. by Jared Sparks, p. 397
11. *The Making of George Washington*, by William H. Wilbur, p. 221
12. *Ibid*, p. 222
13. *George Washington*, Vol. I, by Henry Cabot Lodge, p. 69
14. *The Making of George Washington*, by William H. Wilbur, p. 223
15. *Writings of George Washington*, by Jared Sparks, Vol. XII, p. 145
16. *Field-Book*, by Benson J. Lossing, Vol. II, p. 220
17. *George Washington*, by Henry Cabot Lodge, p. 43-44
18. *Ibid*, p. 69
19. " p. 7

Chapter 6--President Washington Warns the Nation
1. *The Writings of George Washington*, by Jared Sparks, Vol. XII, 1834-7, p. 2-5
2. *Life of George Washington*, by Washington Irving, 1857, Vol. V, p. 21
3. *The Writings of George Washington*, by Jared Sparks, 1834-7, p. 119
4. *The Making of George Washington*, by William H. Wilbur, p. 227
5. *Ibid*, p. 224
6. *International Encyclopedia*, 2nd Ed., Vol XV, p. 135

7. *National Archives*
8. *The Life of General Washington,* by Mason L. Weems, p. 170
9. *George Washington the Christian,* by William J. Johnson, p. 250-251
10. *Eulogies and Orations on the Life and Death of General George Washington,* from *George Washington the Christian,* p. 250-251
11. *Early Sketches of George Washington,* by William S. Baker, p. 74
12. *Character Portraits of Washington,* by William S. Baker, p. 284
13. *George Washington,* Vol. 1, by Henry Cabot Lodge, p.69-70

CELEBRATIONS OF A NATION
BIBLIOGRAPHY

Adams, Samuel, *The Rights of the Colonists*, 1772

Appleton, Cyclopedia of *American Biography, Vol. VI*, 1889

Ashton, Robert, *The Works of John Robinson*, 1851

Baker, William S., *Character Portraits of Washington*, 1887

Baker, William S., *Early Sketches of George Washington*, 1894

Bancroft, George, History of the United States, Vol. II, Third Edition, 1838

Berk, Stephen E., *Calvinism Versus Democracy*, 1974

Boller, Paul F., Jr., *George Washington and Religion*, 1963

Bradford, William, *Of Plimouth Plantation*, 1647

Burk, W. Hergot, *Washington's Prayers, 1907*, from *George Washington the Christian* by William J. Johnson, 1976

Butterfield, L. H., *Adams' Family Correspondence*, compiled by Butterfield

Cambridge of 1776

Carlson, Paul, *Our Presbyterian Heritage*, 1973

Carlson, Paul, Eerdman's *Handbook to Christianity*, 1983

Chaucer, Geoffrey, *The Canterbury Tales*

Commager & Morris, *The Spirit of 1776*, 1958

Conway, Montcure D., *George Washington's Rules of Conduct*, 1890

Custis, George Washington Park, *Recollections and Private Memoirs of Washington*, 1828

Fisk, John, *The Critical Period of American History*

Encyclopedia Americana

Flexner, James Thomas, *American Heritage Series*, Vol. XIX, Dec. 1967, "Providence Rides a Storm"

Flexner, James T. *Washington, The Indispensable Man*

Furneaux, Rupert, *Pictorial History of the American Revolution*, 1973

Foster, Marshall/Swanson, Mary-Elaine, *The American Covenant-The Untold Story*, Ltd. Ed. 1981

Freeman, Douglas Southall, Vol. 4, *George Washington, A Biography*, Vol. 4

Geller, L. .D., *They Knew They Were Pilgrims; Essays in Plymouth History*, Poseiden Books, Inc. 1971

Goodwin, John, *The Pilgrim Republic*, 1888

Guyot, Arold, *Physical Geography*

Hall, Verna M., *Christian History of the American Revolution,* 1976

Hall, Verna M., *Christian History of the Constitution of the United States of America,* 1966

Harland, Marion, *The Story of Mary Washington,* 1892

Hart, Prof. Albert Bushnell, *Washington, Man of Mind*

Hoare, H. W., *The Evolution of the English Bible,* 1901

The Holy Bible

International Encyclopedia

Irving, Washington, *The Life of George Washington,* Vol.I, 1815

Jefferson, Thomas, *The Life and Morals of Jesus Christ*

Johnson, Wilbur J., *George Washington The Christian,* 1919

Johnston, Lucile, *The Space Secret of the Universe,* 1969

Kistler, Charles E., *This Nation Under God*

Lincoln, Abraham, *The Gettysburg Address,* Encyclopedia Americana

Littell, John Stockton, *George Washington the Christian,* 1919

Lodge, Henry Cabot, *George Washington,* 1889-1898

Lossing, Benson J., *The Pictorial Field-Book of the Revolution,* 1886

Marshall, Peter/Manuel, David, *The Light and the Glory,* 1977

Meltzer, Milton, *Milestones of American Liberty,* 1961

Miller, Perry/Johnson, Thomas H., The *Puritans,* Vol. I

Muhlenberg, Henry Melchoir, Notebook of a *Colonial Clergyman*

Myers, Robert J., *Celebrations*

National Archives

Neal, Daniel, *History of the Pilgrims,* 1731

Norton, John H. *Life of General Washington,* 1870

Scheer Rankin, *Rebels & Redcoats*

Slater, Rosalie J., *Teaching and Learning American History,* 1965

Smith, Horace W., *Orderly Book of the Siege of Yorktown,* 1865

Smith, Page, *A New Age Begins*

Sparks, Jared, *The Writings of George Washington,* Vol. II, 1834-7

Stoudt, J. J., *Ordeal at Valley Forge,* 1963

Sweig, Donald M. & Davids, Elizabeth S., *A Fairfax Friendship, The Complete Correspondence Between George Washington and Brian Fairfax,* 1982

Toner, J. M., *Washington's Barbados Journal,* 1751-2

University of Wisconsin, *The Geneva Bible, Facsimile Edition, 1969*

Weems, Mason L., *The Life of General Washington*, 1808
Wheeler, Richard, *Voices of 1776*, 1972
Whitney, David C., *The Colonial Spirit*, 1974
Whitney, David C., *Signers of the Declaration of Independence, Founders of Freedom*, 1964
Wilbur, General William H., *The Making of George Washington*, 1970
Van Doren, Carl, *Benjamin Franklin*, 1938
Whiting, John, Edited by Henry Whiting, *Revolutionary Orders of General Washington*, 1844
Williams, William Carlos, *In The American Grain*

ILLUSTRATIONS CELEBRATIONS OF A NATION--
Early American Holidays